T5-ASQ-342

3⁵⁰

ALBERT SCHWEITZER

by Albert Schweitzer

THE PHILOSOPHY OF CIVILIZATION

I THE DECAY AND RESTORATION
OF CIVILIZATION

II CIVILIZATION AND ETHICS

INDIAN THOUGHT AND ITS DEVELOPMENT

GOETHE

THE QUEST OF THE HISTORICAL JESUS

THE MYSTERY OF THE KINGDOM OF GOD

PAUL AND HIS INTERPRETERS

THE MYSTICISM OF PAUL THE APOSTLE

J. S. BACH

ON THE EDGE OF THE PRIMEVAL FOREST

MORE FROM THE PRIMEVAL FOREST

Adam and Charles Black

MEMOIRS OF CHILDHOOD AND YOUTH

MY LIFE AND THOUGHT

FROM MY AFRICAN NOTEBOOK

George Allen & Unwin

ALBERT SCHWEITZER

The life of a Great Man

by

JEAN PIERHAL

LUTTERWORTH PRESS
LONDON

First English edition 1956

This is a shorter version of
ALBERT SCHWEITZER : Das Leben eines guten Menschen
first published by Kindler Verlag, Munich, 1955

Printed in Great Britain by Richard Clay and Company, Ltd.,
Bungay, Suffolk

Contents

List of Illustrations

LIST OF ILLUSTRATIONS

The photographs of *Kaysersberg* and the *Günsbach* pulpit are re-
produced by permission of Ernst Grossar, Munich; plate 12 by permission
of PA-Reuter Photos; the "high street", Lambarene, and plate 16 by
permission of Pictorial Press; and plates 20, 21, and 22 by permission of
Keystone Press Agency, Ltd.

Acknowledgments

The quotations on pages 76 and 85 from C. T. Campion's translation of *On the Edge of the Primeval Forest*, by Albert Schweitzer, are reprinted by courtesy of the publishers, Messrs. A. & C. Black.

Grateful acknowledgment is made to Messrs. A. & C. Black and to Messrs. George Allen & Unwin for permission to include in this edition a number of translated passages from works by Albert Schweitzer of which they hold the English copyright. A list of books by Schweitzer published in Great Britain appears on page 2.

CHAPTER 1

The Happy Valley

WITH FEET HELD together the young pastor Louis Schweitzer jumped over the tiny cradle, so pleased was he that God had bestowed on him a boy as his second child.

Of course it cannot have been a very high jump, for the rooms in the old Protestant vicarage, buttressed by the ramparts of the ancient little town of Kaysersberg in Upper Alsace, had really low ceilings. On the same day, January 14, 1875, the little bell in the slim turret straddling over the roof as a substitute for a real church tower tinkled with its thin tones as though to mark the general jubilation.

Six and a half months after Albert's birth, the parson's family moved to a new parish, on the edge of cool, thick mountain forests and nestling in fat green pastures and vineyards. The place was called Günsbach in the Münster valley.

This ecclesiastical appointment represented a considerable advancement for Louis Schweitzer. While the Protestants in Kaysersberg had been scattered and in a minority, in this friendly little village of vineyards there was an important Evangelical community where the new pastor was inducted on August 1, 1875.

Pastor Schweitzer had been born about the middle of the century, the son of a schoolmaster in the town of Pfaffenhofen. He had attended the grammar school and university of Strasbourg. But in contrast to his two brothers, who had been drawn to Paris, where, like so many other men of Alsace, they had quickly made careers for themselves, he was content to remain in the beloved province friendly to Protestants which had been the home of the Schweitzer family since the time of their first removal from the Swiss canton of Schwyx during the wars of the Reformation.

The Protestants of Günsbach, like the members of many other Evangelical churches in Alsace, had to grant to Catholics the use of part of their church. Louis XIV had decreed, in an edict of 1686, that in all Evangelical parishes of Alsace which had at least seven Catholic families the choir of the church should be set aside for their worship. In many places this led to friction and quarrels, but never in the half-century in which Louis Schweitzer exercised his pastorate in Günsbach. He had already learnt the spirit of confessional tolerance as a young curate in Mühlbach, not far from Günsbach. His austere and venerable vicar, Pastor Johann Jacob Schillinger, always insisted that there should prevail between the clergy of the two churches a spirit of mutual respect, deference, and constant co-operation. In Mühlbach it had been the custom that the Evangelical pastor should do duty for the Catholic priest in regard to sick visits when Monsieur le Curé was engaged on long journeys. When on one occasion the Protestant vicarage was threatened by fire, it was speedily evacuated and all the effects transferred to the Catholic presbytery. For a long time the tale was told with relish in Mühlbach of how there suddenly appeared in the chaste bedroom of the curé a heap of feminine garments—the crinolines of Pastor Schillinger's wife finding a temporary home!

Adèle, Albert Schweitzer's mother, was a daughter of the Vicar of Mühlbach. The fact that she had him baptized Albert was not without significance. Albert had been a half-brother of Adèle Schillinger, honoured for his extraordinary kindness and readiness for self-sacrifice. He died as the result of an unusually strenuous deed of heroism: in the year 1870—when Alsace was still French—he had fought his way to Paris in order to get medicines for Strasbourg, which was already cut off by German armies. On his return he was taken prisoner by the Prussians. While the general in command allowed the medicines to go through, Pastor Albert Schillinger was detained as a prisoner. Tortured by the fear lest his parishioners should believe that he had left them in the lurch in such distressing times, the heartbroken man began to pine away, and died in 1872, not long after his return home, and in the same year as his father, the Vicar of Mühlbach, who had suffered cruel anxiety about his vanished son.

Toleration, the spirit of self-sacrifice, and also the hatred of war, which had brought so much sorrow to their loved ones, were thus already rooted in the family tradition of the parents of Albert Schweitzer. "The Protestant-Catholic church which arose from the caprices of Louis XIV's absolutism, is for me more than a curious historical phenomenon," Albert Schweitzer wrote later. "To me it affords a symbol signifying that confessional differences will ultimately disappear." He expressed similar hopes in regard to the relationship between those hereditary enemies, France and Germany. Both were to him a fatherland. He always felt their tragic strife, to which not only his uncle Albert was to fall a victim, to be especially painful.

The Münster valley or, as it is also called in Alsace, the "little Switzerland of the Vosges", is one of the most beautiful, fertile, and populous valleys of the Wasgaus.

But the valley has yet another quality which is not usually noted by travellers' guides: it makes its inhabitants happy. For what reason? It may perhaps be due to the mingling of sweet and bitter in the landscape whose fir-clad mountains permit only a scanty Alpine vegetation but whose carpets of grass, vine hills, and shady spreading walnut-trees suggest the rich fruitful life of the temperate climate proper to the plain.

Here in the happy valley where everything glittered, blossomed, and flourished, whether vine-clusters or cows, flowers or cabbages, it was a fact that mostly full-blooded, healthy children were born. Thus it is understandable that the first impression of "Albertle"—a puny child just snatched from death—did not exactly inspire confidence.

The parsons' wives of the neighbourhood, thinking no doubt

of their own rosy-complexioned, chubby-faced angels, became silent with embarrassment when the wife of the newly inducted pastor of Günsbach showed them on that festive occasion her little son, who lay hidden in his pretty cushions as in a sick bed.

"But the milk of neighbour Leopold's cow and the bracing air of Günsbach did wonders for me," Albert Schweitzer later reported.

The happy valley lay somewhat apart from the main routes of traffic. Hence it retained ancient customs and costumes longer than most other parts of Alsace. At the time when young Albert Schweitzer was playing in the garden of the parsonage, the men who visited his father still wore a cocked hat, a long brown coat, a black neckcloth, short grey knee breeches, long stockings, and buckled shoes. Women would put on black protective hoods, black coats, and bodices. They were gloomy colours, suggestive of the tenacity with which people clung to use and habit and the ancient faith. There was of course boisterous merry-making at the weddings and baptisms of these country folk, lasting often a whole week; there were days of high festival when home-brewed drinks were poured out, but such occasions were exceptional. On normal days people ate chiefly potatoes, cabbage, and Münster cheese and the famous Münster valley meat pie, made from meat roasted, and then smoked.

In every farmhouse were to be found centuries-old Bibles and pious books, and even in the upper stretches of mountain pasture, inhabited only in summer by milkers and dairy lads, the holy book was always part of the most essential equipment. No meal would have been complete without a prayer for blessing at its beginning and an expression of thanks at its end, and there was no week which was not consecrated and enriched by Sunday worship.

The new pastor soon made himself greatly beloved by his flock. He lived in a damp old house, but was never heard to

The pastor's family: a group taken when Albert, standing in the centre, was ten years old. (*Below*) Albert (marked with cross) at the village school at Günsbach, 1880. The organist Iltis is on the right

Schweitzer's grandparents, Pastor Schillinger and his wife. It was from his grandfather that Albert was thought to have inherited his gifts as an organist

complain. He was always on the spot with help and advice, and in his preaching, unlike some others, he did not conceal an ignorance of life behind a knowledge of learned phraseology, but spoke simply out of the depths of personal experience. "I am at heart a layman," he used to say. "But He"—pointing to a portrait of Christ—"was also a layman, not a clever theologian!"

When Pastor Schweitzer preached, his little son was always in the congregation. How often he could not help yawning! Then the maid would place over his mouth her work-coarsened hand, clad in its Sunday thread glove, or would give him a little push so that he should not fall asleep and thus set a bad example to the other parishioners.

But when the congregation sang he was most alert and would join in lustily. He loved music; it gave him a thrill of pleasure or a cold shiver of awe.

Only one thing disturbed his boyish enjoyment of the music. As soon as his father had left the pulpit and the thunderous organ-tones boomed forth, then there appeared aloft looking over the instrument a shaggy face. It seemed to the boy to be making grimaces at the congregation. There could be no doubt about it—it must be the devil.

"Satan looks down at us every Sunday morning during the service. Didn't you know that, Papa?"

The figure whom little Albert thought to be Satan was the village organist, whose face rose phantom-like in the mirror over the organ every time he sat down before the manuals. But during the half-hour occupied by the preaching of Pastor Schweitzer he did in fact disappear. During that time the organist used to perform his Sunday toilet: he shaved carefully, then trimmed and curled his hair, unmindful that the preacher below him was denouncing the vanities of this world.

That vision of the "devil" sent many a cold shudder down Albert Schweitzer's back. When works of edification were read of an evening round the fireside of this country parsonage, and the question of Satan was brought up, Albert was sure that he knew him personally. But why was it that no one else seemed to have seen Satan? He often pondered on this. Was it that he himself was perhaps specially wicked? Was he the only person to have seen the prince of hell bodily?

He had many other similar causes of distress. There was the maid who in the mornings would try to tame his bushy and rebellious child's hair with comb, water, and pomade. She succeeded only with difficulty and often hardly at all. Then she would rebuke him soundly and affirm that he resembled his hair—undisciplined, self-willed, and perverse.

He gained consolation, however, on the occasion of a visit to the museum in nearby Colmar, where he saw the Isenheim altar. The sight of this work of art powerfully affected him— not because he had precocious insight into its artistic greatness, but because with a glow of delight he noted in it how rough and bristly was the hair of John the Baptist.

There was also the story about horns growing on the forehead which made him afraid. Monsieur Jägle, an old fellow who filled with dignity the office of sacristan and gravedigger at Günsbach, let slip no opportunity of teasing and frightening the pastor's little boy. He would feel the lad's high forehead and murmur: "They are growing, your horns are growing. They will soon be through."

While the father allayed his son's fears, he could not altogether dispel them. Meanwhile the gravedigger served up a new hair-raising idea.

"Now we are ruled by the Prussians, *mon petit*. Some time you will have to become a soldier like all men. Then the smith will measure you for a suit of iron."

Albert began to watch the blacksmith's shop on the other side of the street, but not a single soldier ever came out of the workshop encased in iron. It was a puzzle to know what to think of grown-ups. Did they really speak the truth or did they always tell lies? And if the latter, why did they lie?

CHAPTER 2

Boyhood Days

LOUIS SCHWEITZER took his duties more seriously than many other pastors. He cared not only for the welfare of the soul but also for that of the body among his flock. The poor, the unfortunate, and the bereaved could always count upon him. He took them fruit from his garden and often gave them something from his small stipend as well.

In order to earn a little, and also out of a desire to write, the pastor contributed to the *Church Messenger* and sent village stories to the almanacks. He gave accounts of quarrels among the country folk, and of true love, abandoned maidens, illegitimate children, and local intrigue. His story of the bottle of champagne which saved the life of a dying person, his Alsatian Romeo and Juliet which he called "In the Meadows", and the short story, "Kattel's Christmas Tree", full of tender feeling and, at the same time, some social criticism, made the name of Pastor Schweitzer well known beyond the boundaries of his parish. His model was Jeremias Gotthelf, the Bernese Swiss pastor with the powerful pen, and if he himself did not attain the same literary mastery, yet the country life of those days is faithfully and agreeably portrayed in these moralizing fables.

He also found time to give his son Albert a grounding in the essentials of piano-playing. Music was as natural in this parson's family as prayer. Both Albert's paternal and maternal grandfathers had been organists in their spare time. Grandfather Pastor Schillinger, who had ruled his family and his parish of Mühlbach in strict and patriarchal fashion, became far more tender and approachable when he had sat for a time at the organ.

The pianoforte in the Günsbach parsonage was the bequest of Grandfather Schillinger, and on it Albert Schweitzer was taught by his father. When a schoolmistress jingled out an accompaniment during the school hymn practice he offered to point out to her how it should be done, climbed on to the piano stool, and struck up the right harmonies. With astonishment he noted that the mistress continued to play wrongly even after this correction by one of her pupils. For the first time he perceived that he could do something which others could not do.

It was a special thrill when for the first time he chanced to hear two-part singing. This happened to him twice a week when he waited with his class in front of the classroom of the older pupils, whom the master was taking for a singing lesson. Through the closed doors he heard such songs as "Down in the mill I rested peacefully", or "Sweet forest, who possesses you". In his rapture he had to hold on to the wall. "The thrill of part-singing sent a shiver through my whole body," he wrote later concerning this experience.

The photos of the time show a rather sulky-looking fellow, suspicious and always on the watch, ever ready to defend himself. His reserve he seems to have inherited from his mother, to whom he was bound by a close, almost silent relationship. He himself says that he derived his passionate and fiery temper from her and Grandfather Schillinger. Even as a child he took everything that he did with the utmost seriousness. He tolerated no joking even in games. At the age of nine or ten he blamed his sister Adèle severely "because she was a lax opponent in sport".

Nor did Albert Schweitzer as a boy eschew fighting. One day on the way home from school he challenged his schoolfellow, George Nitschelm, who was bigger than he and considered stronger.

A circle soon formed around them. They threw their satchels away, took appraising looks at each other, circled around each other cautiously in search of the best point of attack, and then suddenly hit out, to the loud applause of the school onlookers. At first it seemed as if the bigger boy with the superior weight of his body would knock over the smaller one without any difficulty, but Albert with a groan released himself from George's grip, and suddenly had him down. They struggled on the ground until George clearly touched it with both shoulders. Beaten, he hissed into the face of Albert Schweitzer, "Yes, if I could have meat soup twice a week like you, then I would be as strong."

That day Albert crept home like someone who had received a sound thrashing rather than one who had floored the biggest boy in the class.

"But why are you not eating your soup?" asked his mother, who knew her son's appetite well. "Don't you like it?"

He stared at her with his big eyes, but said nothing, and silently poked around on his plate. On no account would he touch a spoonful of this hated dish. To himself he swore, "I am going to be like the other boys. I will see to it that I differ in nothing from them."

It was an impossible oath and one destined to cause him much suffering. The boy now strained every nerve to imitate the other boys in everything. He insisted on wearing the same cap as his school comrades instead of the sailor one that had been chosen for him, and to the annoyance of his parents he refused to put on the fine new coat that had been specially cut for him out of the material of a cape of his father's. Not even the scolding and punishment his father gave him could induce him to wear this coat.

On visits to his godmothers Barth or Patin in Colmar the boy allowed himself to be persuaded into various pranks, which afterwards caused him sharp pangs of conscience. There was the piano trick, for example. Albert would act as a substitute player for a friend who found piano-practising very tedious. While she read an exciting book Albert would do her practising, a little trick which often succeeded, until the girl's mother, astonished at her daughter's progress, came into the room to listen. There, throned at the piano, was young Schweitzer, while her daughter lay on the floor devouring her book.

He once feigned severe toothache in order to compel his father to take him to the Colmar dentist. Albert had heard of the marvels of Monsieur Schwartz's surgery and wanted to see for himself. The dentist saw through the innocent fraud and commented laughing on the boy's healthy teeth.

Another adventure of his boyhood was his escapade of sailing on the forbidden River Lauch at Colmar. But none of these boyish experiences affected Albert Schweitzer so permanently as his first sight of one of Colmar's public monuments.

There stood in the Champ de Mars of Colmar, within a small park, a monument to the French Admiral Bruat, who had made himself famous by his colonial conquests in the service of his country. Although Alsace had belonged to the German Empire since the end of the Franco-Prussian War, the authorities in Strasbourg and Berlin—more tolerant than a later German government—had allowed this monument to French national glory to stand untouched.

The boy was powerfully attracted by this memorial statue. Originally it was no doubt his youthful enthusiasm for the sea which had drawn him towards the monument of a hero of the Navy. But it soon became clear that the rather stout gentleman with the peaked cap who seemed stranded up there on the plinth interested him less than the form of a negro who lay with bent head at the foot of the monument.

The sculptor Bartholdi, a native of Colmar who was later to become famous as the creator of the American Statue of Liberty, had, in carving the form of this negro, produced an extremely striking piece of statuary. The muscular giant, so strong, yet so subjected, so free from the trivialities of civilization with which the admiral towering above him was so richly furnished in the form of medals, epaulettes, and sword, and yet plunged in such deep dejection, increasingly absorbed the attention of the Günsbach boy.

The village street at Günsbach: Schweitzer's house is on the right

Kaysersberg in Upper Alsace, where he was born

In the garden at Günsbach, 1893. Albert Schweitzer is on the left

Schweitzer's mother with her sons Albert and Paul, 1905

"In the face and bearing of this Herculean giant form of the negro there lay a melancholy which pierced my heart and moved me to reflect on the destiny of the black races," Schweitzer later recollected. "Every time when we were going to or from the station through the Champ de Mars I requested that we might make a detour past the statue in order that I might greet the negro and converse with him. During my schooldays in Mülhausen I remained faithful to the custom of going to visit my black friend hewn in red sandstone whenever I was in Colmar. From 1896 onwards . . . I had many opportunities of visiting Colmar to renew my knowledge of the town, to see old friends and gain new ones, to enjoy the lovely chimes of the bells of St. Martin's—and finally to be with the negro. Bartholdi's statue first conveyed to me the idea of the African mission which later I fulfilled."

If the melancholy of the statue of a negro helped to invoke the boy's compassion, the forgiving smile of a pedlar taught him to be patient and tolerant. The name of this pedlar was Mausche. He dealt in domestic utensils, but also bought and sold farmers' cattle and land. As a Jew, he was forbidden by law to settle as a farmer or a trader, and it was traditional among the Günsbach children to regard Mausche as a figure of fun. Hardly was his donkey seen trotting along pulling the loaded cart, when the village oafs would come running out to tease the pedlar. They pushed pinafore ends twisted into the form of a pig's ear under his long nose, and assailed him with showers of abuse.

"But he went forward," says Schweitzer in *Memoirs of Childhood and Youth*, "as calmly as his donkey. He just turned round at times and smiled kindly and with an air of embarrassment. Mausche taught me for the first time what it is to be silent under a storm of persecution. He became indeed one of my great teachers."

Albert even grew accustomed to taking Mausche's arm and accompanying him through the village out on to the bridge which spanned the rivulet Fecht.

One of his first great moments of insight now began to

dawn. "I must not blindly imitate others, merely in order to put myself on good terms with them," he said to himself. "Whenever my innermost conviction is involved, the opinion of others will be indifferent to me, even though such independence brings me into ridicule. I must overcome all fear of ridicule. I will free myself from the fear of men."

Like many children Albert Schweitzer had from his earliest years almost as close a relationship with animals as with men. Every evening when his mother closed the door and he lay in the dark, the boy murmured his childish prayer. He put his hands together and once more saw them all clearly—the people he had met that day: his father with his big black beard, his mother whose face was so thin and drawn, his elder sister and younger brothers and sisters, the postman, the other boys, and the woman next door. He had already prayed for all of them. But there was also the dog Phlox, and the old narrow-chested beast of the neighbouring wagoner, and the cows which grazed in the meadows, and the butterflies and the bees and the storks, which were especially fond of making their nests on the roofs of Alsatian houses, and the pigeons and swallows. His thoughts went out to his special friend Fritz in Colmar. Fritz was one of the thirty cart-horses belonging to Mühlebeck the carrier; with the carrier's daughter, the boy loved to build stalls for the horses out of boards. Fritz was blind, yet he went bravely on dragging the heavily loaded beer wagons through the rough streets of Colmar. Ought one not to pray for him, above all?

Thus the child thought of all his friends when he closed his prayer with these words: "Dear God! Protect and bless everything that has breath, keep them from evil, and may they sleep in peace."

He was once enticed by another small boy to go catapulting birds. Afraid of being ridiculed as a milk-sop if he refused to go, Albert took his catapult, fastened into it a sharp pebble, and took aim. Just as that moment the church bells of Günsbach rang out—which seemed to be the voice of heaven. He flung away his catapult, jumped about shouting to scare the birds, and then rushed home. Two of Albert Schweitzer's great decisions were made there on the hillside above Günsbach—one, not to kill living creatures, and the other to have the courage to act on personal conviction.

CHAPTER 3

On the hard School Bench

ALBERT SCHWEITZER was nine years old when his father felt that he could no longer properly be kept at the village school. He would have preferred to send his son at once to the classical school at Mülhausen, but that was some distance from Günsbach. Had Albert gone there at this stage it would have meant an immediate separation from his home for the period of his future school life. His father realized how much the sensitive boy would suffer by such a sudden banishment from the bosom of his family. Hence he found a temporary compromise. He resolved to send Albert for a year to the secondary school at Münster.

It was a wise decision, for in this way the boy gradually accustomed himself to attending school away from home. But, above all, the journey of two miles to school furnished him with new experience. Here, in the shadow of the blossoming cherry-trees, the lime-trees in summer, the chestnut-trees in autumn and the bare wintry slopes of The Gallows—a mountain as sinister as its name suggests—Albert Schweitzer for the first time encountered the full range of Nature's beauties. He tried to express his feelings in poetry and to sketch the old castle ruins in the background. Neither attempt, however, would stand the test of his early-developing critical faculty. Usually his pen came to a stop after two or three rhymes, and after a few strokes he would throw away his pencil in despair.

"From that time on I gave myself up to the pure visual enjoyment of beauty without trying to elaborate it in artistic form," he wrote later in *Memoirs of Childhood and Youth*. "Up to the present I have never again attempted to express myself in art or poetry. My creative bent has come out only in musical improvisation."

When, after a year of this schooling, the stern decision could no longer be postponed to send the boy to the classical school at Mülhausen, there was much heartbreak and many tears. Even now it would be difficult for Albert to catch up with the other boys in the second form.

"Schweitzer," the master at the desk repeats, more loudly, with an emphasis on the vowel. A boy with close-cropped hair jumps up from his seat in confusion, and stands out in the narrow gangway between the benches.

"Now would you please have the goodness to tell us why Goethe has used the word 'ruh' in this poem?"

The pupils titter over the hypocritical politeness and the mocking deference which the teacher uses only when he is about to catch an inattentive pupil. Schweitzer remains silent. He does not even attempt to mumble something, as other boys in a similar position would do. How can you tear a poem to shreds so mercilessly? It is like cutting up a living being. As soon as the torment to his feelings had begun he had simply turned his attention away from the lesson, and instead of listening he began turning over the pages of a reading-book.

"Well, Schweitzer?"

The boy presses his lips tight and stares with his big eyes at the teacher. He doesn't even apologize. His conduct is most irritating. Were he not related to the Mülhausen school inspector, thinks the master, one might proceed very differently with him.

A few days later the headmaster asked the boy's father to come and see him.

"Pastor, I am sorry to have to tell you that your son will not be promoted if he continues to be so inattentive and dreamy."

"He is homesick, headmaster."

"Well, in that case he would do well to go back to his former school. In my opinion he is not really suitable for a classical school. In these circumstances how can I feel really justified in keeping a place for him?"

"Please have a little patience with him," the parson asked in some humiliation.

"Right; but you must give him a real scolding for once."

That, however, the parson did not do. He thought that sort of thing unimportant, and also he probably knew instinctively that not much would be gained thereby in the case of his thick-skulled lad.

Only gradually did Albert Schweitzer begin to improve. He grew more accustomed to the gloomy official residence of the childless great-uncle who lodged and boarded him during his time at school. He accepted the pedantic discipline which prevailed in the household, the strict daily time-table on which his aunt punctiliously insisted—a mode of life which seemed to acknowledge only work and the performance of duty. Great-uncle Louis, now inspector of all the elementary schools in Mülhausen, had been in an earlier stage of his career the head of a Franco-German institute in Naples, and like his wife Sophie had brought back with him an insuperable repugnance to anything easy-going.

Hence everything in his house, on the upper floor of the central school in Mülhausen, was organized according to an inflexible daily programme. Hardly had Albert got up from his midday meal when he had to practise the piano, then there was afternoon school, and as soon as he got home again the order was, "Get down to your homework." When he had finished the last stroke of his pen in the evening, his aunt urged him back to his Czerny exercises.

Where were now the walks in the forest? the leisured strolls over the vine-covered hills? Here in this struggling industrial town one hardly noticed the passage of the seasons. The fresh green of spring, the full flush of summer, the red tints of autumn were all merged into the greyish gloom of printed paper, the changeless black of the type. It was terrible to be so cut off from the life of Nature. His very comfort came from dreams of memory and hope.

Albert Schweitzer himself ascribes his eventual improvement in his studies to a new master whom he learned to love and admire.

As master of the third division in the classical school at Mülhausen, Dr. Wehmann at least understood how to interest his pupils and how to give them a pattern of self-control. Not only did he cause the work and reports of his pupil to improve considerably within three months, but he inspired in Schweitzer the fundamental realization that only he who lives up to his ideals himself can exercise a genuine influence over the lives of his fellow men. This teacher of the classics transformed the twelve-year-old boy into a better-than-average pupil.

About this time his uncle and aunt took him to his first concert. Marie-Joseph Erb, an Alsatian who had achieved prominence in Paris as a composer and pianist, gave a piano recital one evening in the Exchange Hall at Mülhausen. Almost everyone in the rich provincial town had dressed up for the occasion. Never had the village lad seen so many ladies in evening dress, or so many gentlemen in dinner-jackets and dress-coats. He tried to make himself as inconspicuous as possible, for he was ill at ease: he had long grown out of the Sunday suit which he was wearing that evening. But the noise which the audience made surprised him even more than their pompous attire—hundreds of voices in conversation, programmes rustling, and crackling sweet-bags being passed round.

Hardly had the pianist begun to play when the boy was thrilled by the solemn emotion which so far he had experienced only when hearing church music. He was still quite enthralled when the first enthusiastic applause began. He sat motionless among the clapping people, and while his neighbours were chattering away again, rattling papers, and handing round sweets in their silly, empty-headed way, there still ran through his head the music he had just heard.

"Didn't you like it, then?" someone asked him.

He nodded silently with only the faintest inclination of the head.

"But why didn't you clap?"

Again he was silent, with lips pressed tight. What did the music really matter to these dressed-up people who could not even express their gratitude for the beauty and greatness of what they had heard by the tribute of silence?

Not even his piano-teacher realized how much music meant to the growing boy, how the world of sound was for him the true, ideal, divine creation, not yet distorted by evil.

"Schweitzer is my headache," Eugène Münch was accustomed to say when speaking of his various pupils. Münch, a deeply religious man, who loved to "pray" for many hours a day on his organ (for that is how he would have described his solitary organ playing), was considered to be a distinguished music teacher, but his art seemed to fail when applied to Albert Schweitzer. The boy, many of whose forebears were organists, should have had hereditary gifts. Yet, seemingly bored and with a wooden touch, the boy used to strum off his exercises. He would make a wretched tinkle out of one of the finest sonatas of Mozart. Then his teacher, usually so aloof and sensitive, would lose patience. One day he gave the boy one of the *Lieder ohne Worte*, and remarked, "It really isn't any use giving you beautiful music to play. I'm afraid you'll spoil even this. If a man has not feeling, he can't interpret the music properly."

At the next lesson, after the usual finger exercises and studies had been gone through, the pupil closed his eyes, settled himself into a good position on the piano-stool, and played Mendelssohn's *lied* as he felt it within himself. Deeply moved, Münch understood without any further explanation. He slapped Schweitzer on the shoulder, and responded to this act of musical confidence spontaneously and appropriately by beginning to play himself. In the *Lied ohne Worte* as Münch played it then there was an infinity of meaning which he dared not utter in any other way. Ridiculed for his shyness, Münch

The road from Günsbach to Münster

The sorrowful negro of the Colmar statue, which made such a deep impression on Schweitzer in his boyhood

...nur wenige Stunden mit Stephan Zweig zu verleben
...war mir vergönnt. Wir haben sie beide ausgekostet.
...wie nach dem ersten Zusammensein schieden war es
...uns, als hätten wir uns schon lange gekannt. Das letzte
...Mal war ich mit ihm zusammen in England in seiner
...schweren Zeit vor dem zweiten Kriege. Da ermaß ich, was
...er unter der Heimatlosigkeit erlitt. Fortan gedachte ich seiner
...in steter Sorge.

Albert Schweitzer

Albert Schweitzer's handwriting, and his school report for the year 1893

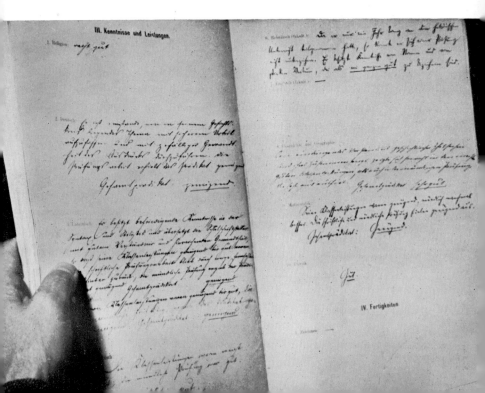

was at last able to pour himself out to Schweitzer; and thus began a friendship which lasted until Münch's sudden death.

Gradually the boy's stiffness began to melt. He became more inclined to talk, and even began to judge his harsh relatives somewhat more sympathetically. Ever since the day when, in a gentler moment, his aunt had understood the meaning of his yearning gaze out of the window, and had without a word taken him for a walk, he had ceased to regard her as a prison wardress whose sole delight it was to drive him to the piano and restrain his boundless passion for reading.

On the other hand, Schweitzer's openness of mind, his keen interest in everything, his countless questions, his surprising doubts about accepted ideas, soon became a torment, and appeared most suspicious to some people. He was a tireless questioner. There was no lunch-hour whose peace was not disturbed by his habit of posing problems and splitting hairs, no supper which he did not make uncomfortable by his many probing questions. If this sort of thing had been confined to the intimate family circle, it might have been acceptable. But wherever he went, alone, or with relatives or parents, he seized the first opportunity to begin an argument. His patient father made him promise to leave at home this awkward behaviour during conversations, but it was unavailing. He could not be silent.

When, through the teaching of his revered headmaster Wilhelm Deeke, he became acquainted with Platonic philosophy, he was happy to note that a famous thinker of antiquity thoroughly confirmed him in the incivility of this inexhaustible passion for criticism. Like a young Socrates, he now sought to draw the citizens of Mülhausen into a discussion of eternal problems. He would stand about even in midwinter in his thin light brown suit, and ply all and sundry with his endless questions. But the citizens of Mülhausen were by no means Athenians, they would leave him standing and hurry on about their business.

It was his great-uncle who most of all had to suffer from his eager questing mind. Young Albert loved to draw him into political debate. Questions of the day, such as the struggle of the Prussian Government with Rome, and the laws against socialists, Bismarck's dismissal, the Reichstag speeches of Eugen Richter, the complications of the Balkan wars, and colonial politics were fiercely discussed in the sombre official residence.

He was concerned, too, about colonial peoples. Among his earliest memories was one of his father reading aloud the recollections of Casalis, the French African missionary. Schweitzer cherished an admiration for the silent heroism of this messenger of the Gospel. But the coarse, massacring heroes of colonial warfare who, with their gunboats, compelled the capitulation of men quite helpless against these new weapons, and who forced them to accept the more than doubtful protection of the national flag, inspired him with little respect.

Such opinions were hardly calculated to make the youth popular at that time. For public opinion referred with pride to the white man's burden. The new shops for colonial wares which were springing up brought even into small towns a reflection of the splendour of these exotic adventures. In order to excite interest in the parts of the earth inhabited by the coloured races, whole negro villages were sent from place to place like a sort of wandering circus. Such a group visited Mülhausen during Albert Schweitzer's schooldays. The report of one school year notes that the boys, under the supervision of their masters, had gone to see the Wakamba negroes, for all the world as if they had been to gape at a menagerie.

The political debates round the supper-table, which bored Aunt Sophie, had originally begun because his aunt had tried to forbid Albert to read the newspapers.

"You only devour stupid love stories and murder stories, of course," she had asserted, annoyed because, instead of helping to lay the table he rushed to read the *Neue Mülhauser Zeitung* or the *Strasburger Post*.

"That isn't true," answered Albert. "I read particularly the political part, and politics is really nothing other than contemporary history. . . ."

"We will soon see about that," interrupted his uncle. "Who are the reigning princes on the Balkan thrones at the present time?" The inspector was thoroughly in his element. Even with his napkin round his neck, and facing a plate of roast potatoes, he remained the experienced examiner.

The answer came like a pistol shot from the other side of a still higher pile of roast potatoes.

"Good. Now something more difficult. What, then, are the names of the prime ministers and cabinet ministers in the last two, or shall we say three, French governments?"

Again the answer was not only free from error but so exact that the questioner himself could hardly have equalled its accuracy. When the boy had reported most intelligently the arguments in recent Reichstag debates and had expressed views about them, his examination success was complete. Albert was allowed to read the newspaper not only before but even after supper.

Things did not always go off so smoothly for Albert Schweitzer. In the school-leaving examination things very nearly went wrong, and that not because of his sins, but because of his virtues. The fact was that he had wanted to spare his parents the expense of the regulation dark examination suit. He was able to procure a dark coat from a distant relative of similar size, but the trousers which went with it were not delivered. So at the last moment he borrowed the official dress trousers belonging to his uncle, who must have been a corpulent and portly but only middle-sized gentleman.

The result of this hastily put together outfit might have succeeded with the judges of a fancy-dress ball, but was hardly suitable for the solemn occasion of a *viva voce* examination. The rather nervous and depressed air of the six other examination candidates was transformed into explosive gaiety as soon as Schweitzer appeared, and the gaiety increased when he related how he had lengthened his braces with tapes so that the trousers would reach at least roughly to the edge of his boots. But, as Schweitzer himself said, "This could not prevent white space showing above the top of the trousers. I will not describe how they appeared from the back."

While there was still a patter of good advice on all sides, and while everyone was laughing at their clownishly dressed comrade, the door of the examination room opened. To their amazement, the gentlemen of the teaching staff, solemnly attired and seriously minded, and headed by a chief inspector of schools specially brought from Strasbourg, found, instead of the usual line of worried-looking examination candidates in the dismal corridor, an extremely merry company. The school staff very soon understood the reason for this merriment, and could hardly conceal a smile themselves.

In the centre of this unusual group stood the candidate Schweitzer. The chief examiner decided to have him in and deal with him privately. Schweitzer was unable to answer many difficult unprepared questions simply because his teachers had not dealt with the topics, and he resigned himself to being ploughed. Then, happily, the ferocious examiner came in conclusion to his own special line, and Albert's special study—history. After ten minutes there arose an almost friendly conversation on a matter that was dear to Schweitzer's heart: the colonization methods of antiquity. The report on his certificate was "very good" in history, "good" in physics; otherwise mostly only "satisfactory". Even the German essay, a paper in which Schweitzer usually shone, was not very well done this time, in the opinion of the examiner, although the subject set sounds like a motto through the whole life work of Albert Schweitzer: "For his good, man is a child of sorrow."

CHAPTER 4

The Student and his Masters

A MOST ELEGANT young man, with a thick, rebellious crop of hair, like that of the new fashionable philosopher Friedrich Nietzsche, and a fresh growth of moustache, which made him appear older than his eighteen years, stood leaning on his walking-stick at the exit of the Gare de l'Est in Paris, and for the first time in his life looked expectantly at the passing life of the French capital.

It was Albert Schweitzer, who had recently left the Mülhausen classical school, the future student of theology and philosophy, whom his father's two wealthy brothers—August Schweitzer, the well-placed Paris banker, and Charles Schweitzer, the distinguished German philologist at the Sorbonne—had invited to come to Paris.

In the late summer of 1893 Paris had just acquired a new feature—the iron tower of Monsieur Eiffel, whose peak reached far higher into the heavens than the towers of Notre Dame—criticized by some as heathenish and by others as a grotesque expression of human vanity.

"What can we show you?" asked his relatives, who once more got to know their Paris through the wondering eyes of their country nephew.

"Everything," he answered uncertainly, and apparently without much conviction.

"And what would you especially like to see?"

"Ah, there I don't think you will be able to help me. Not even Eugene Münch, my organ-master, has dared to give me a letter of introduction to this man."

"Who, then, is this formidable person whom you desire to see?"

"Widor," said young Schweitzer—"Charles Marie Widor, the composer and organist."

"But that won't be so difficult," Aunt Mathilda declared, to everyone's surprise. "It so happens that I know him— rather well, in fact. Although he was born here in France, he is of Hungarian extraction. Strictly speaking, he is even half Alsatian. His grandfather, who was an organ-builder, lived not far from your home at Günsbach."

She sat down at once and wrote out a letter of introduction in her neat hand.

It was not fear but awe which moved the young man as he made his way through the narrow streets of the Left Bank towards the church of St. Sulpice. He had never yet stood in the presence of an acknowledged master of any particular subject. Would he stand the test, or would he be robbing the master of something more than his time? He had wanted so much to be allowed to play the organ before him. Perhaps he would even ask him for instruction. But as he drew nearer and nearer to the church where Widor received friends and pupils every day at a particular time, he slackened his pace, chose by-ways, and stood hesitating in front of the shops which sold priests' vestments, crosses, chalices, and statues of the Blessed Virgin. He browsed aimlessly among the open book-chests of an antiquarian dealer.

But from the towers of St. Sulpice the hour boomed out. In he went, knocking far too loudly on the door on which was a visiting-card bearing the honoured name.

"*Entrez!*" thundered a voice from the other side of the door. The irrevocable step had been taken. With a flushed face and an agitated heart, Albert Schweitzer presented himself to the great Charles Marie Widor, whose artist's room was adorned with signed photographs of famous contemporaries, and precious engravings. Slowly—much too slowly, it seemed to Albert Schweitzer—Widor read through the letter of recommendation.

The master was elegantly dressed, and wearing a blue-and-white-spotted Lavallière cravat. He was not so old as Schweitzer had imagined—at most in the late forties. And although different, no doubt, he somehow seemed to resemble Albert's music-teacher, Eugène Münch. The impression was probably due to the look of aloofness from the world which good organists wear on their brows as a sign of the spirituality of their calling.

"Well, young man?" asked Maitre Widor, "what would you like to play to me?"

"Bach, of course," was the brusque answer.

"Good! Let us go."

They climbed up to the gallery, to one of the most famous organs in the world, the work of Aristide Cavaillé-Coll.

Widor sat down before the three-manual instrument, explaining keyboards, registers, and pedals, pulling out the flute and bourdon stops, and giving a demonstration of the *voix celeste* with its heavenly sweetness, almost as if he already had a pupil before him.

"Now, young fellow."

Albert Schweitzer closes his eyes. His gaze is turned inward. His wildly beating heart is stilled. Fear and awe of the man beside him have vanished. His whole attention is concentrated on the work of the cantor of St. Thomas's, Leipzig. He begins to play the A major fugue—that work of Bach's which he himself wanted to inscribe with the title "the joyfulness of faith", and already the two strangers—the young Alsatian at the beginning of his career and the Parisian master at the height of fame—meet in those fields of heavenly music.

Is there now any question whether Charles Marie Widor will take the young man as a pupil? The question is not even put. It is already answered.

"So the day after to-morrow I will see you here again," says Widor to Schweitzer as they go back to his room. "How long are you going to remain in Paris?"

"Unfortunately, only three weeks. Then my university career in Strasbourg begins."

"What a pity! In that case you must come to me to-morrow morning. Don't let us neglect a single day."

And again Albert Schweitzer stands on the square in the shadow of St. Sulpice. And everything—the tramways, the bright-coloured dresses of the ladies, the whirling maple leaves on the ground, the posters, and the light feathery clouds —all belong to the great and glorious symphony of fulfilled life which opens up before him.

At the beginning of the academic year he took up residence at the theological seminary of Strasbourg, the Collegium Wilhelmitanum—which lay in the shadow of the church of St. Thomas. Here, in one of the simply furnished rooms which looked out on to the swiftly flowing green waters of the Ill and the pleasant ivy-clad garden with its conventual calm, stood a narrow bed, a simple table, bookshelves, and, as a special favour of the principal, a piano with an organ pedal-board. In the future every other work-room of Albert Schweitzer's was to follow this austere pattern.

He plunged into his studies with furious zeal. His intellectual ardour was unquenchable. For long hours he sat at the feet of such men as the theologians Holtzmann and Budde, the philosophers Ziegler and Windelband, the music theorist Jacobstal. From time to time, although he had not signed on for such lectures, he attended courses in the Department of Natural Science, for he was well aware of the vast importance of the new scientific discoveries, and even bitterly regretted that he had left school with an inadequate knowledge of chemistry, physics, geology, and astronomy.

Of course music especially must not be neglected. Soon Schweitzer had struck up an intimate friendship with Ernest Münch, the noted brother of the organ-teacher of Mülhausen. Gottfried, the third of this trio of brothers, was likewise studying theology in the seminary, and so the two "Wilhelmitanians" would sometimes sit up until the early hours playing duets together.

With his wife Helene, 1913. They were married on June 18, 1912

Eugene Münch, Schweitzer's music master during his schooldays. (Right) The student, 1895; the following year Schweitzer made his great decision

At the same time Albert Schweitzer enjoyed the usual student pleasures of drinking beer and dancing. He always turned up with the same eager good humour. He was popular with everyone on account of his musical gifts, his sense of fun, his sweetness of temper, and, last but not least, his prepossessing appearance. His charm was irresistible.

Albert Schweitzer was hardly ever alone at this time. He took part enthusiastically in the rehearsals and performances of the St. Wilhelm's church choir conducted by Ernest Münch. Months before a performance, Schweitzer and the Münch brothers would sit round a table of an evening discussing the programme, a big edition of Bach spread out before them, from which they chose suitable cantatas. If only they could play and sing them all! But four must suffice for the next concert. Then for Albert began the task of copying out the score, for their budget was not sufficient to enable them to buy printed copies.

If it was a question of drafting advance notices of the concerts for the Press, the task was allotted to Schweitzer, and it was he who cajoled the church treasurer into giving them extra credit for rehearsal work or music paper.

"However do you manage to do so much?" his fellow students asked him.

Usually he only laughed. But if they pressed him, he showed them a poem cut out of a French calendar, which he had framed and hung up above his work table.

> Higher, ever higher,
> Let thy dreams and wishes rise,
> Let them mount like flame of fire,
> Upwards to the skies.
>
> Higher, ever higher,
> And when thy heaven is overcast,
> May thy star of faith aspire
> Till all is bright at last.

For more than sixty years this extract from a calendar was

Schweitzer's inspiration. It is still to be found, faded, above his writing-desk in Günsbach.

One fine morning in 1894 an unusual sight presented itself to the citizens of Strasbourg. A young soldier, curiously equipped, was marching rapidly, in fact running rather than walking, through the narrow streets of the city. Wherever he went bursts of laughter and head-shaking greeted him.

A prominent doctor, who was known to be friendly to the French, and who, since the annexation of Alsace by the German Empire, had kept all his windows darkly shuttered, declared: "I prefer the Kaiser's soldiers like this than with Prussian spiked helmets!"

Another more practical person suggested: "If you only stand here and gape and say nothing, the young man will get a week's detention for a breach of discipline. For heaven's sake, soldier," this man shouted, "go back. You can't go on parade like that."

Albert Schweitzer stood bewildered, looked down at his blameless uniform, put his hand to his head, and, flabbergasted, found that he was wearing a straw hat.

This rather arbitrary uniform, half civilian, half military, really suited the one-year conscript Albert Schweitzer far better than a regular uniform would have done. Schweitzer has often said that he took very little trouble over his soldiering. Nevertheless from April 1894 till April 1895 he did his twelve months military service like all other young men. Happily he had a very understanding superior. Captain Krull often allowed Schweitzer to leave barracks after the day's routine, to return to his monastic little study lined with books, and to be away until midday the next day. On the days when Windelband lectured, Schweitzer, instead of being at the disposal of the Prussian State, was allowed to listen to what the eloquent Professor had to say about the ideal state of Plato.

When there were field exercises outside the town such special treatment became impossible, but even on manœuvres

Schweitzer would take every opportunity of withdrawing himself. He had a Greek New Testament in his knapsack, and as soon as the troops rested anywhere he would take out the small black-bound volume and begin to read it. Often when the other soldiers were so tired that they could hardly keep awake, Schweitzer would sit as usual poring over his Bible. After specially gruelling marches this was a feat of endurance which gradually compelled recognition and respect from those who mocked at him.

It was not only industry that drove the nineteen-year-old youth to such intensive Biblical study. It was the same passion which had driven him when an older schoolboy to accept nothing as a matter of course, to think out and examine carefully everything that he heard, saw, or read, as though no one before him had been occupied with the subject. He now turned on the Gospels his eagerness for radical impartial criticism and his desire to reach independent conclusions.

One day, lying in the grass when he was on leave in the little village of Guggenheim, and reading over the eleventh chapter of the Gospel of St. Matthew, there came to him in a flash an insight which he did not dare to formulate at first, but which ultimately he was unable to reject. It was the observation that if a certain text in the tenth chapter of St. Matthew's Gospel were correctly interpreted, Jesus was there announcing to His disciples an event which did not actually happen. He predicted to them much persecution and the imminent coming of the supernatural Kingdom of God. But they did not experience such events.

The recruit brooded over the problem.

"How comes it about that Jesus holds before His disciples the prospect of things which according to the continuation of the Biblical narrative do not come to pass?"

It occurred to him of course that Professor Holtzmann had an explanation pat. He used to maintain that this prediction of the Lord to His disciples was not historically trustworthy and that in all probability it was introduced later.

"But," the young doubter in his uniform greatcoat again queried, "why should later Christians have placed words in the mouth of their Master which, as they perfectly well knew, had not been fulfilled? That is very improbable; surely that won't do."

Was it possible that the highly esteemed Professor Holtzmann had made a mistake in his interpretation? Very understandably the nineteen-year-old student of theology shrank from supposing any such thing. What right had he, a beginner, to doubt the judgement of a man so highly esteemed in the whole world of scholarship? But why not?

Still more serious was the next conclusion which Schweitzer's mind found irresistible: "Hence it would appear that Jesus did not proclaim a kingdom which He and His disciples were to found and embody in the natural historical world, but one which was to be expected in the forthcoming supernatural age."

When, a few months later, Schweitzer, as a student of one year's standing, was very gently examined in a Bible-reading tutorial by that same Professor Holtzmann, about whom he was beginning to have such serious doubts, he did not yet dare to express his new conclusions, which threatened the whole structure of Protestant Biblical research. He felt downright ashamed when confronted by the kindness of this teacher, who could not have the smallest suspicion that the student, years younger than himself, sitting opposite to him, was not only an admiring pupil, but also the shrewdest critic of his whole life's work.

From this time on Albert Schweitzer was no longer to be seen in the lecture-rooms as often as during his first year. Instead he sat at almost all hours of the day surrounded by high piles of books in the college or university library. His capacity to read a book quickly, which his Aunt Sophie had always blamed in him, now stood him in good stead.

Schweitzer thought he had discovered that official theology, out of respect for religious tradition, had apparently not fol-

lowed the historical data concerning Jesus with scrupulous
fidelity, and, as he put it, instead of allowing the historical facts
to speak for themselves, "had dealt with them in such a way as
to evade their impact, to get round them, or conceal their true
bearing". So now with fiery eagerness he studied the Holy
Scriptures in order to find confirmation of his theory.

In so doing he was disturbed by the realization that his thesis
might prove most painful for the Church, which in any case
was just then depressed by the general tendency to secularism
and materialism.

"Have I the right to cause unrest and disturbance?" he asked
himself when in the late night hours in his little room in the
seminary he outlined a rough draft of his future theological
work. And the answer came to him in a memory of some
words of St. Paul which had been familiar to him from earliest
childhood: "For we cannot do anything against the truth, but
only for the truth."

That thought gave him new strength and confidence. No
doubt he sometimes seemed to himself like the restorer of a
picture. He set to work patiently to remove layer after layer
of daubing with which subsequent generations had coated it,
in the hope of eventually revealing at its base the genuine and
true portrait of the Son of Man.

The same impulse to discover scientific truth was about that
time manifesting itself in all minds of the highest order. The
discovery of X-rays by Röntgen in the year 1895, of radio-
active Becquerel rays by the French physicist of that name in
1896, and Rutherford's treatise published in the same year and
entitled *Of the Nuclear Structure of the Atom*, called in question
centuries-old accepted truths concerning the nature of matter.
In 1895 Freud published his first momentous conclusions which
shook all previous understanding of the human psyche.
These were the years in which the announcement of Carl
Ludwig Schleich about his successful experiments with local
anæsthesia set a medical congress in an uproar; the first natural-
istic dramas of Gerhart Haupmann were hissed off the stage in

derisive merriment; and the whole intellectual world trembled from the blasts of dynamite administered by the philosopher Nietzsche.

But, above all, deep rents in the structure of society became visible for the first time and gave a presage of future revolutions: the poverty in which millions still lived was, and could no longer be accepted as a matter of course. On all sides people were becoming troubled about the disfigurements in the face of contemporary civilization, but it often seemed that while much was said about social conscience and responsibility, very little was in fact being done to relieve the distress of the poor.

It was hardly surprising that Albert Schweitzer, who as a child and youth had felt so keenly the suffering of animals, should be deeply stirred now, when he saw with his own eyes the misery of the lower classes, in cities like Strasbourg and Paris. It was really no wonder, he thought, that the so-called proletariat should cease to be interested in the Church. Had the Church given *them* its full and sympathetic attention? The future pastor made himself felt not merely in seeking the historical foundations of Christianity but also in laying his finger upon the gaps and dissimulations in the practice of Christian charity.

With a breath of relief Albert Schweitzer used to escape from Strasbourg whenever, on Sundays or holidays, there was a chance of going back to his parents' home in the rectory of Günsbach. There, in place of the worries about money and health, for the last few years there had been a reasonable degree of comfort and well-being. A distant relative had left the rector her small means, and a Günsbach resident had bequeathed his fine and convenient house to the parish, so that the rector might at last have a suitable dwelling, instead of the old dark, damp house. The pastor's poor health quickly improved after this, and, since the burden of her cares had been lightened, his reserved, austere wife had shown a quite new serenity and cheerfulness.

How bright the rectory seemed, with the mauve wistaria

round it, when Albert and his friends came dashing home on bicycles. Then the dining-room table would be pulled out, for the young people, who looked so ascetically serious when they were discussing the problems of the universe in the rectory garden, brought with them very keen appetites, which were sharpened by the smell of cooking and of the real Alsatian "mashed cakes" coming from the kitchen. If the eldest son came home with rather too many of these lean-looking young men, or if relatives from Mühlbach or friends from Münster were also of the company, then a long table was laid in the courtyard. Of course every guest wrote his name in the visitors' book, on the front page of which was inscribed: "Forget not hospitality, for many have entertained angels unawares."

To the clergyman's great embarrassment his sceptical brother, the Parisian banker, wrote underneath: "The devil has entered into others," with such violent strokes of the pen that in spite of all attempts on the part of the parson to erase it, the saying was still plainly to be read.

It was a tradition in the rector's family that on Sunday afternoons they should take a walk with all their guests, domestics, and animals to a little meadow just behind the village. In spring everything was in bud, in summer the broad grass and flower-covered slopes were in full bloom, in autumn the paths dotted with burst chestnuts, motley vine leaves, and the soft light brown foliage of walnut-trees, in winter it was as if this little valley had become luminous with the erect snow-white fir-trees.

In the evening there was music; the piano was played and they sang in parts. The rector read to the company his latest story for the almanack, and at midnight Albert would climb on to the stool of the church organ so that the whole party might strike up as a grand finale, "Now thank we all our God."

On the morning after one such splendidly full day—it was at Whitsuntide of the year 1896—there came to the twenty-one-year-old theological student Albert Schweitzer as he lay in bed the illuminating thought: "My good fortune is great. My home is ideal. I am allowed to study at the university; I can even accomplish something as an artist and can enjoy many beautiful things. I am healthy and strong. But can I really take all this as a matter of course? May it not be that the lightning-flash, which last April struck the house of God in Günsbach and nearly destroyed the organ, was intended as a warning to me?"

As so often before, he worried his head about the misery of the world which held so many in thrall. Bestow upon them something of the fulness of one's happiness? That was surely what one should do? Serve, not merely reflect and talk? Really take the initiative to help the suffering, and do so with all one's might? Jesus said: "Whosoever will save his life shall lose it; but whosoever shall lose his life for my sake and the gospel's, the same shall save it."

But then doubts occurred. "What will my parents say, who have sacrificed so much for me, if now I give up my studies in order to devote all my energies to the poor and heavy laden? What will my well-wishers and friends think of me, who expect from me great things?"

And the voice of the Master answered:

"When you prepare a feast, do not invite your friends or brothers or neighbours, who are rich enough to return your hospitality. Invite rather the poor, the halt, the maimed, and the blind."

"But I cannot tread this difficult path at once," confessed Albert Schweitzer. "I am still too young. First of all I would like to know something of the great joys of life. Until my thirtieth year I will live in the service of knowledge and art. After that I will give myself wholly to the wretched, to those who are condemned to walk in darkness."

Having taken this decision, he got up from bed. On that fine spring morning Albert Schweitzer was gayer than any other member of the pastor's large family and their guests, but he disclosed to no one his new plans.

In minister's gown and bands outside his house at Günsbach, 1930

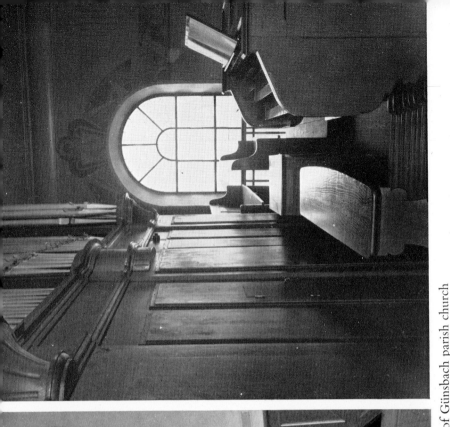

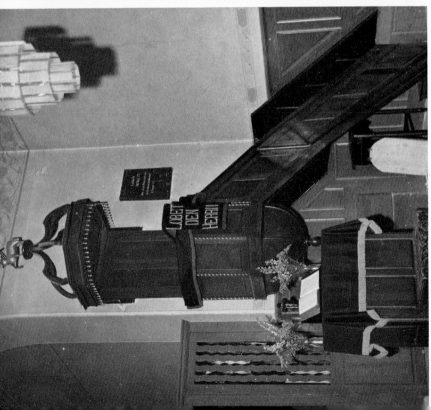

The pulpit and organ of Günsbach parish church

CHAPTER 5

Nine Restless Years

"I SIMPLY CAN'T understand the fact that we admired him so little. Many a time he had to defend himself with all his might."

In these words Elly Heuss-Knapp, later the wife of the President of the German Federal Republic, described the attitude of his closest friends to Albert Schweitzer in those Strasbourg years when he was growing from youth to manhood. On that Whitsuntide morning of the year 1896 he had allowed himself nine years to devote to the perfecting of his knowledge and his artistic talent. Nearly a whole decade in which he aspired to learn and to teach, to read and to write as much as another man would do through a whole lifetime. Then, from his thirtieth year onwards, he would no more belong to himself, but would give himself to the fulfilment of another and higher task.

Yet no one but himself knew of his secret decision, and so to other people the many-sided and restless activity of the Günsbach parson's son seemed odd, in fact plainly suspicious. He appeared to be a Jack-of-all-trades.

For in those days no one supposed that this burly country youth would bring to fruition the many things which he undertook at once. The fact that he only just got through the oral examinations which he had to undergo from time to time apparently justified those who shook their heads doubtfully. On the other hand, it was usually said that Schweitzer did remarkably well in his written tests. He handled in a highly original fashion the subject which was set as a thesis for the public theological examination, namely "Schleiermacher's doctrine of the Last Supper as compared with the interpretation furnished by the New Testament and the confessions of the Reformers", and moreover the talk was that his treatment was based upon thoroughly sound scholarship.

Hardly had Schweitzer passed this first theological examination when he plunged headlong into the study of philosophy. In the summer of 1898 he had to give up, for the time being at any rate, his much-loved room in the seminary. As chance had it, the lodgings which he took in the Fischgasse had been occupied a century previously by none other than Johann Wolfgang Goethe.

He was spurred on by the fact that on the recommendation of his teacher, Professor Holtzmann, he received the Golsch studentship worth 1,200 marks a year. The donor of these emoluments had made it a condition that the elected student should either take the degree of licentiate in theology within a rather meanly short time or pay back the money he had received during the prescribed period. Anyone else would either have shied off at the harsh conditions attached to this stipend, or else have felt incited to press on to the attainment of this second important theological degree within the year allowed for preparation. Schweitzer did nothing of the sort. To the surprise of his friends, he seemed to put aside his theological studies altogether for the time being. Instead he took upon himself a new line of study. He pressed his philosophy professor, Ziegler, to suggest to him a theme for a doctorate dissertation in philosophy.

On the steps in front of the university under the protection of Ziegler's enormous black umbrella something like the following conversation might well have developed:

"Do you want to be a theologian or a philosopher, Schweitzer?"

"Both, Professor. For, after all, is not the knowledge of God ultimately consistent with the world views of the great thinkers?"

"The majority of my colleagues would deny it, but you are fortunate in that I too was originally a seminarist and theological student at Tübingen. Perhaps my background there would give me something to say precisely on this debateable issue. How would it be if you went rather closely into the religious philosophy of Kant?"

"Gladly, Professor. You know my preference for the philosophy of the eighteenth century."

"One more question, Schweitzer. Are you not overdoing things a bit? Do you ever get any sleep?"

"Sleep, Professor? Isn't that comparatively unimportant?"

At that time Albert Schweitzer enjoyed such robust health that he was almost able to do without sleep. From October 1898 he was in Paris officially as a student of philosophy at the Sorbonne, but in fact much more occupied with his third line of study—music.

When he left his room early in the morning for an organ lesson with Widor, his bed was often still undisturbed. Sometimes, after a social evening, he got back to his lodgings at eleven o'clock, or even midnight, and at once lit the study lamp and settled himself to read until the early hours of the morning. Then, after a quick cold splash in a hip-bath in the early morning, he would gulp down strong coffee at the bar of the nearby bistro along with men on their way to work.

In spite of all the exertion involved, Schweitzer felt himself astonishingly fresh. Widor himself had no suspicion of his favourite pupil's sleepless nights. As ever, Schweitzer was alert and good-humoured.

Sometimes a rather elderly gentleman in a skull-cap, who rarely spoke, was present at these organ lessons. He watched the playing both of the younger and the older man attentively. While they talked he gently stroked the console with an almost caressing gesture. This was the great organ-builder Aristide Cavaillé-Coll, one of those devoted craftsmen to whom the perfection of their handiwork means more than any profit. If even the smallest detail of an organ did not quite please him or his fellow workmen, he would take the whole structure to pieces and begin again, until the desired perfection was attained.

But the new age no longer had much use for such expensive carefulness. Monsieur Cavaillé-Coll had time to listen to his patron Widor and the young Monsieur Schweitzer so often because he could find so few customers now. Everyone seemed to want ever bigger and more powerful organs, built in factories, and furnished with all sorts of new gadgets which by their technical tricks made fifteen stops sound as marvellous to the uninitiated as fifty stops on the older and more solid instruments. The three organ-lovers constantly spoke of this regrettable new tendency.

That not all new discoveries are good, that modern developments, in spite of the increase in knowledge and ability, do not always spell progress, but often imply retrogression and even decadence and imminent destruction, was a conviction which forced itself on the mind of Schweitzer during those last years of the nineteenth century. This view, so utterly opposed to the optimistic spirit of the time, with its delight in progress, first became fully clear and irresistible to him in the autumn of 1896, when, on his return from the Bayreuth festival, he stopped at Stuttgart in order to hear the new organ in what was then the "Hall of Song"—an organ praised at the time as a masterpiece of contemporary organ-building.

But when Lang, the organist of the abbey church, introduced Schweitzer to this seventh wonder of the world he was shocked. The new instrument was indeed powerful and loud, but the effects of the various stops mixed together confusingly. Schweitzer's fine ear heard only a chaos of sound. "The thin reedy sounds drown the full diapasons, just as the lean kine of Pharaoh ate up the fat kine," he thought. "A well-played organ should be like well cooked rice. Just as in a good dish of rice you can taste every granule, so you should be able to distinguish clearly every sound on a good organ." What a horrible mess was served up from this instrument!

From that time on Schweitzer fought against the roaring in-flated "music machines", first in conversation, and then in letters and petitions on behalf of the old unspoiled organs.

"I sacrificed much time and energy in this struggle for the true organ", he wrote later in *My Life and Thought*. "I spent many a night over plans for organs which I had to give an opinion of or retouch. I undertook many journeys in order to study questions of organ repair or rebuilding on the spot. The letters which I wrote to bishops, cathedral provosts, presidents of consistories, mayors, clergy, church councils, church elders, organ builders, and organists amount to hundreds and hundreds. . . . And how often so many letters and journeys were in the end useless because the people concerned decided after all on the type of organ which sounded so well on paper.

Schweitzer did not stay a full five months in Paris at that period. In spite of his concentrated subordinate preoccupation with music, and his lively participation in the intellectual and social life of the French capital, when he returned to Strasbourg in the middle of March 1899 he had in his trunk his completed doctorate thesis. It was a work of more than three hundred pages. Vexed at the bureaucratic slowness with which the *Bibliothèque Nationale* in Paris functioned, he decided after a few visits to its great reading-room to read nothing of the previous work that had been done on the theme of his dis-sertation—the religious philosophy of Kant—and instead to study more deeply the original text of Kant's works. This laboriously precise piece of textual criticism enabled him to make the discovery that Kant had woven into his famous *Critique of Pure Reason* an earlier study in the philosophy of re-ligion. This interesting thesis, which showed his power of lively and independent thought, won the unqualified approval of Professor Ziegler, who proposed to its author that at the end of the summer term he should submit it for examination.

After receiving such a favourable report from his philosophy professor, Schweitzer was impatient to leave Strasbourg in the April of 1899. Before taking the official doctorate examination he wished at last to visit that other capital city of Alsatians—

Berlin. It was a journey upon which he set out with eager
curiosity, but also with some misgiving. Berlin, the capital
city of the German Empire, aroused in him, as in so many
other Europeans who lived west of the Rhine and south of the
Main, both respect and mistrust, for there were conspicuously
manifested two of the most dubious achievements of the new
age: nationalism with its pride in armed strength, and the
boundless optimism of a society which was elated by its
industrial progress.

In fact the young pastor's son at first found in Berlin what
he had expected: an astringent positive atmosphere, in which
men were judged above all by their actual achievements, and,
interwoven into this stern militarily disciplined rhythm of life,
the fanfares of regimental music, the rigid, almost machine-
like steps of marching troops. It all sounded like an overture
to the twentieth century, on which the curtain was shortly to
be raised.

But alongside this self-consciously ambitious Berlin there
was another Berlin—the Berlin of the thinkers, poets, men of
letters, musicians, and creative artists, and this Berlin was more
reflective, less madly and thoughtlessly optimistic. Schweitzer
encountered this aspect of the city too, for the organist of the
Kaiser Wilhelm Memorial Church, Professor Reimann, introduced him to circles of this kind; but it was above all the widow
of the Hellenist Ernst Curtius who in her salon brought him
into contact with the leaders of German intellectual life.

On one of those lovely Berlin summer evenings a company
was gathered in the home of Frau Curtius. As the long summer
day declined to its end, with the antique sculptures of the late
professor casting their long black oppressive shadows over the
assembled guests and on the backs of the lines of books stretch-
ing up to the ceiling, someone out of the deepening twilight
was heard to exclaim: "Alas, after all we are nothing but decadent epigones."

The word at once inflamed the mind of Schweitzer. All the
criticism and opposition to the movement of the times which

had been piling up in his mind during the last few years caught fire. Epigones—decadent descendants, miserable administrators of a great intellectual inheritance—this is what for some time he had felt his contemporaries to be without having been able to formulate his insight in clear terms.

> From that evening in the house of Frau Curtius I was inwardly occupied amongst my other tasks with a work which I proposed to call "We Epigones",

wrote Schweitzer later in his *My Life and Thought*. He added:

> Sometimes I gave my ideas on the subject to friends, but as a rule they took them only as piquant caricatures and manifestations of a *fin de siècle* pessimism. Consequently I kept quiet about the whole matter.

Thus once again the young Albert Schweitzer was at cross-purposes with his environment. Very few men were anxious like himself about the future of mankind in the century now dawning. "Anyone who expressed doubts was looked upon with astonishment," reported Schweitzer when in the year 1921 he cast a retrospective glance at that time.

> Some who were on this wrong path, paused and went back again on to the great high road, because they were getting anxious about these devious ways. Others continued to walk in them, but silently. The insight which was at work in them doomed them to loneliness.

At heart misunderstood, unappreciated and isolated—that is the picture of Albert Schweitzer, despite his whirl of activity, which the nine restless years of apprenticeship and travel from 1896 to 1905 suggest. Certainly judged from a purely external point of view his career seems distinguished enough, in fact brilliant. He had got through his *viva voce* for the doctorate thesis and the newly minted doctor was encouraged by his professor to become recognized as a university lecturer.

Schweitzer, however, decided in favour of theology rather than philosophy, "which leads such an enfeebled impoverished existence", and he accepted a post as curate at the church of St.

Nicholas. This was where his late uncle Albert, after whom he was named and who had been his mother's favourite brother, had preached. At the same time he prepared for his next theological examination, worked in his former room at St. Thomas's lying on the floor surrounded by piles of books as he researched into the Last Supper and the life of Jesus; played the organ in St. William's church; began, at the suggestion of Widor, an essay on Bach, which unexpectedly grew longer until it assumed the dimensions of a book; delivered in 1902 his first lectures as a recognized teacher at the University of Strasbourg, and from October 1903 assumed office as head of the St. Thomas's Seminary (Collegium Wilhelmitanum), in which he had until recently lived as a student.

All these were successes which could make him justifiably proud and which somewhat took the wind out of his critics' sails. And yet they did not make him happy. Was it not simply words, words, words? What was the use of this whole pursuit of culture when in reality the far more important task awaited him—that of warning the world by pointing to and analysing the decay of culture, and, more important still, the task of doing something about it: but how?

Sometimes, but not often, Schweitzer broke silence and spoke about his inner anxieties. That happened above all in the sermons which in his capacity as curate he preached on behalf of the two elderly ministers at the St. Nicholas Sunday afternoon services. Then he spoke about decaying morals in human life, about the ever-increasing dehumanization of man, which he thought was evident in all the phenomena of public and private life. Such addresses were valuable but mostly short, and also a little above the heads of the congregations, accustomed as they were to mild comforting commonplaces. In any event, complaints reached the vicar about Schweitzer. Pastor Knittel felt obliged to speak to his curate on the subject. But there was a small circle of Schweitzer's pupils and friends who regarded his sermons as something quite new and inspiring, stimulating to thought and spiritual renewal. They used these ecclesiastical discourses as the point of departure for many a discussion in the hospitable home of Professor Knapp, who was at home once a week, from two to four on a Saturday afternoon, to the friends and companions of his daughter Elly.

One day Schweitzer noticed that a certain young lady was always present both at his sermons and the subsequent discussions, and that, though apparently much stimulated by them, she never spoke.

"And what is *your* opinion of my sermons, Fräulein Bresslau?" Schweitzer inquired challengingly of this silent watcher.

"From the point of view of style they leave much to be desired," she answered dryly. "Your German sounds as clumsy as if it were literally translated from the French."

So began the story of Albert Schweitzer and Helene Bresslau.

CHAPTER 6

The Great Decision

ALBERT SCHWEITZER and Helene Bresslau had known each other for some time before Schweitzer asked her—four years his junior—to concern herself with his dialect-riddled German. But up till then there had been no intimate contact between them.

For this they were really too divergent in background. Helene Marianne Bresslau came from the capital. She was born in Berlin, and had been brought up there until she reached the age of eleven. Her father, Harry Bresslau, already famous as a historian in specialist circles throughout Europe, came of a distinguished Jewish trading family, but, like so many Jews of the upper middle class, he had had his daughter baptized. Since he was a pioneer of documentary research into the German Middle Ages and a tireless collaborator in the *Monumenta Germaniae Historica*, Harry Bresslau believed that he and his family would always be regarded as good Germans, and no doubt from motives of patriotic enthusiasm he had had himself transferred to the frontier university of Strasbourg, whose cultural mission it was to subdue the still very strong French influences. So much the more painful it must have been for him and his daughter when the children of the Prussian officers garrisoned in Strasbourg angrily taunted the dark-eyed child with cries of "little Jewess".

Helene Bresslau and Albert Schweitzer met for the first time in an almost deserted Protestant church in Strasbourg, where Schweitzer was accustomed to practise the organ. As a young student teacher she was there, too, rehearsing hymns with a Sunday-school class. When the silvery tones of a variation on a theme of Bach's echoed through the church she was probably struck by the clarity of the playing, by the calm masterly perfection of the execution, and thus her interest in the invisible organist was aroused.

Originally, Helene Bresslau, like her school friend Elly Knapp, had wanted to become a teacher. She had distinguished herself as a pupil at the Linde Girls' High School, which was under the headship of a keenly intelligent and large-hearted woman. At the age of eighteen she passed her examinations at the teachers' training college, and subsequently had taken only temporary teaching posts, preferring to give her full attention to the study of music at the town conservatory. A rather long stay in Italy with her parents, during which Professor Bresslau was rummaging about in Upper and Middle Italian archives, inspired her with enthusiasm for painting and sculpture. She then decided for the time being to give up the idea of an eventual permanent teaching post and began to study the history of art in Strasbourg.

In the autumn of 1902 she crossed the Channel to England to take up a position as governess. When she returned to Strasbourg in the following year, a fundamental transformation had taken place in her. Enthusiasm for music and art and the striving after higher culture receded, and she was preoccupied with social questions to which her eyes had been opened in the manufacturing towns of England. So on January 1, 1904, she began a course in nursing with the evangelical deaconesses.

This decision was destined to have a revolutionizing influence on the life of Albert Schweitzer. Refusing to be seduced by the ever-increasing recognition he was winning as a critical theologian, he had not for one moment lost sight of his resolution to serve the Gospel from his thirtieth year by beneficent action, instead of by words and writing. One of his favourite ideas was to offer to orphan and neglected children something of the warm-hearted and generous upbringing which his own parents had given to him. Why should he live alone in the college principal's bright, spacious lodgings? Could he not bring up a few abandoned children there? He called on the director of the Strasbourg orphan's home, but found that official regulations prevented this.

There were also the tramps and discharged prisoners. Schweitzer got into touch with these by offering to relieve the friendly pastor Ernst of St. Thomas's church of some part of his charitable work. But again no avenue of service opened up.

It was then that Schweitzer read the story of Henry Chapuis, the mechanic of Geneva, who died in his native city in May 1904 at the age of twenty-eight, as a result of a disease contracted as an artisan missionary in the tropics. Chapuis had been sent out to the Ogowe River area in Central Africa. Hardly a year after his arrival he had been obliged to send his wife and small child back to Europe, as they were unable to stand the climate of Equatorial Africa. Soon after that he, too, became aware of the symptoms of his own fatal illness. Shaken by fever, he returned to Europe on leave, only to die there in silence and obscurity, like so many other missionaries before him.

One of the leaders of the Paris Missionary Society, Pastor Alfred Boegner, wrote an obituary notice for the Society's green-covered magazine for 1904, and added to it the following admonition:

> New resources and energies must be found for the small army which is fighting on the banks of the Ogowe. Where are we to find this new man-power? . . . Where is the young pastor or student who has just completed his training who is willing to give to our brothers on the Congo the strengthening of his help and his youth? May this call find its way to the hearts of those who read it. May the spirit of God Himself pierce the consciences of those . . . on whom already the gaze of the Master rests. . . . The missionary Coillard once related how impressed he was on seeing with what readiness the subordinates of a great African king got up at his mere gesture and came forward with the simple word: "Sir, I go to do your bidding." The church needs men who at the sign of the King of kings answer simply: "Lord, I go: send me."

In the autumn of 1904 the obituary notice and challenge fell under the eyes of Albert Schweitzer when he returned one day to his old student room in the St. Thomas Seminary. He had almost mechanically turned over the pages of the little magazine which Fräulein Scherdlin, a missionary worker, had left on his writing-table, as she had done so many times before. He read, and as the words sank into his consciousness he suddenly felt certain that they were meant for him, quite specially for him. He was seized by no sudden excitement, but rather an unusual peace settled upon his mind. He did not jump up, but remained sitting in his chair as though now released from all disquiet, and set about the work which he had proposed to do that evening.

"My search is ended," he said to himself.

Henry Chapuis had found a successor.

January 14, 1905: the Principal of St. Thomas's College is celebrating his thirtieth birthday. In the early morning the students have congratulated him in the refectory in word and song. To-day his favourite dishes are to be found on the menu, and in his post he finds greetings from the great men with whom he has become acquainted on his journeys to Paris and Berlin; there are also touching letters of thanks from students who have been given courage for their examinations by his last-minute coaching, and the clumsily written gaily decorated letters of some children to whom he gives religious instruction. To-day he would like much to be at home with his parents in Günsbach, but his duties keep him in Strasbourg.

Nine months pass before his great decision is made public.

In the autumn of 1905 Schweitzer went to Paris as usual to see relatives and friends. And there everything seemed to conspire to dissuade him from the project which he had secretly planned. Widor expressed his enthusiastic approval of the manuscript entitled *Bach—Musician and Poet*, which was now ready for the press, with a dedication to his aunt Mathilda.

The master assured his pupil that this work would bring him international fame. A new friend came to greet him in his poet's quarters in Montparnasse: Romain Rolland wished to become more closely acquainted with the organist who had performed so outstandingly at the musical festival in Strasbourg last May.

But at last the day came. On October 13, 1905, Albert Schweitzer posted a number of letters in a blue pillar-box in the Avenue de la Grande Armée in Paris. They were very brief. The sender informed his relations and closest acquaintances that from the start of the university winter term, which was due to begin in a few days, he proposed to take up a course of study in medicine, since he later intended to offer himself as a missionary doctor in tropical Africa. When the envelopes, one of which contained his resignation from the position of Principal of his theological college, slid through the thin slit, he heaved a sigh of relief: at last the irrevocable step had been taken. At last another stride forward had been made.

Helene Bresslau was probably the only person who at once understood why Schweitzer was renouncing the brilliant career opening up before him, and why he wished to make his contribution to the world first and foremost as a doctor. In fact she could even claim that by her own recent choice of a vocation she had considerably helped him towards such a decision. But others, both relations and friends, felt that they could not do enough in their efforts to bring the misguided man back on to the right path. Their sympathy with and admiration for Schweitzer were genuine. They wanted very much to make clear to him the madness of his plan and to warn him of its evil, unconsidered consequences.

"A general—and that is what you are, *cher ami*—does not occupy himself as an ordinary infantryman in the firing line," rumbled Widor.

"If you really want to help the natives, then you would do much better to give lectures on the question. Nowadays it is propaganda rather than action which gives the first impulse to all great achievements," suggested one of his shrewder acquaintances.

Schweitzer explained his decision in particular detail to Gustav von Lupke. This fine music critic had spoken of Schweitzer's French work on Bach in terms of the highest praise in his magazine *Kunstwart*, and had recommended that it should be translated into German. In a letter to him, Schweitzer set forth the reasons for his action in the following clear and convincing words:

> I hope you will give me the pleasure of showing a deeper insight than most people . . . and that you will find the course I am taking as natural and right as I do myself. For me the whole essence of religion is at stake. For me religion means to be human, plainly human in the sense in which Jesus was. In the colonies things are pretty hopeless and comfortless. We—the Christian nations—send out there the mere dregs of our people; we think only of what we can get out of the natives . . . in short what is happening there is a mockery of humanity and Christianity. If this wrong is in some measure to be atoned for, we must send out there men who will do good in the name of Jesus, not simply proselytising missionaries, but men who will help the distressed as they must be helped if the Sermon on the Mount and the words of Jesus are valid and right.
>
> Now we sit here and study theology, and then compete for the best ecclesiastical posts, write thick learned books in order to become professors of theology . . . and what is going on out there where the honour and the name of Jesus are at stake, does not concern us at all. And I am supposed to devote my life to making ever fresh critical discoveries, that I might become famous as a theologian, and go on training pastors who will also sit at home, and will not have the right to send them out to this vital work. I cannot do so. For years I have turned these matters over in my mind, this way and that. At last it became clear to me that the meaning of my life does not consist in knowledge or art but simply in being human and doing some little thing in the spirit of Jesus . . . *"what you have done to the least of these my brethren you have done to me."* Just as the wind is driven to spend its force in the big empty spaces so must the men who know the laws of the spirit go where men are most needed.

CHAPTER 7

Professor into Student

IN STRASBOURG ITSELF, of course, everyone got to know the extraordinary story. It was soon known that in October 1905 Albert Schweitzer, the Professor of Theology, had given his name to Fehling the surgeon, the Dean of the Faculty of Medicine, and applied for matriculation as a medical student.

The story was so fantastic that it went the round of the German universities. In fact, a similar case had nowhere yet been met with, and a complicated technical question arose.

Since he was a member of the teaching staff of the university, Albert Schweitzer could not at the same time be matriculated as a student of medicine. But if the theology professor attended the lectures of his colleagues simply as a visitor, then those lectures could not officially be counted and he could not be admitted to examinations.

There was, of course, the possibility that he should give up his theological professorship. But the university senate would not hear of such a thing. Thus only one course remained open to the senate, which in the event decided that in the special case of Schweitzer it would suffice for his medical colleagues to furnish him with certificates and testimonials concerning the lectures which he had attended. The medical professors for their part very generously resolved to admit their colleague from another faculty without charge.

In fact the medical faculty gradually began to feel themselves honoured to have at their feet such a pupil as Schweitzer. For while in Strasbourg people still spoke with a touch of mockery about the crazy man who was not satisfied with the two doctor's caps for philosophy and theology, in the outside world

Albert Schweitzer was, if not famous, at least becoming very well known. In Paris his recently published work on John Sebastian Bach had created a sensation and given birth to a sort of Bach cult. Still louder were the repercussions aroused by his highly significant book, *The Quest of the Historical Jesus*. The revolutionary scope of this work was particularly realized in the Anglo-Saxon world, while the German theologians, although admiring the author's industry and penetration, could not accept this very disturbing dissertation unreservedly. Meanwhile the man whom prominent people like the Queen of Roumania, the Archbishop of Canterbury, the French poet Romain Rolland, and the widow of Richard Wagner expressed a desire to meet was grinding away in a crammer's class with his fellow students, who were ten to twelve years his junior, and going through questions and answers in science papers.

He would often disappear from the lecture-rooms for three or four days, sometimes even for a whole week, for a music tour in Spain. What Schweitzer confided only to the narrowest family circle was his surprise at the uproarious enthusiasm which his concerts in Spain never failed to evoke—the applause of thousands, the general keenness, and the outstandingly good notices. It was a foretaste of great fame to come, but it was hardly congruous with the modest circumstances of his life in Strasbourg, the sordid shifts to which poverty reduced him, for money had become tight since the beginning of his medical career.

Schweitzer had refused to give up his preaching duties at the church of St. Nicholas along with his principalship. Nor did he fail to deputize at times for his father in the pulpit at Günsbach or in confirmation classes. Once more he was overloaded with work and duties to an almost unendurable extent. He would write sermons on railway journeys or during tedious lectures. He used to memorize his physiology and pathological anatomy during the intervals of choral rehearsals, he would work at his lectures on the doctrine of St. Paul between the various courses of a meal, on a railway station bench, or, as of old, in the late hours of the night.

But he was no longer so toughly resistant, so youthfully resilient, as ten years before in Paris. He lived surrounded by a haze of tiredness which was but seldom dispersed. He could not prevent his eyes closing in broad daylight; he would grow drowsy over his midday meal.

Writing a German version of his book on Bach was a heavy strain on his physical resources. Originally Schweitzer had intended simply to translate the book into German word for word. But he found he could not do this. He found he had far too many new thoughts simply to be able to repeat himself in another language. And so he rewrote, extended, and modified this work on the Leipzig master to such an extent indeed that—to the terror of the publisher—the German version became almost half as long again as the French original, and comprised no less than 844 pages.

But his chronic tiredness never permitted him to taste the full fruit of any one of his successes. He laments in a letter to the musicologist von Lupke:

> I had so much looked forward to enjoying the publication of the book; now I am too tired. So it has been with me throughout my life whenever I had the prospect of some particular joy. And I used to enjoy so much talking to friends, writing to friends, and now all this must be cut down. Don't forget that I am a preacher and that therefore the holidays are no rest for me. And it is hard to preach with a tired and heavy head. . . .

During Schweitzer's medical student days, Helene Bresslau decided to accept a municipal post as a welfare worker among orphans. She was soon known all over Strasbourg. Helene was so very different from the ordinary harsh type of orphan guardian. Intelligent, good-humoured, and affectionate, she quickly dispelled the distrust and softened the stubbornness of many orphan children. She realized that even the most self-sacrificing work of a guardian cannot replace the real love of a mother. Whenever Helene went to the town maternity home to bring away an illegitimate baby and take it to the home for orphans, she tried to persuade the mother to keep the child, and at whatever cost in self-sacrifice to bring it up herself—a suggestion nearly always impracticable, as there was no home in Strasbourg for unmarried mothers and their babies.

But at that time the city had a mayor with a keen sense of social questions. Under Dr. Schwander's administration all social-welfare work was completely reorganized. Hence Helene Bresslau had no difficulty in winning his approval of her plan for the building of a new home in which unmarried mothers could be sheltered and looked after with their babies until they could care for their children independently. In March 1907 an appeal to the townspeople of Strasbourg was launched, organized by Helene Bresslau, with the triumphant result of a collection of 15,000 marks, and a house into the bargain.

Schweitzer himself was also busy on a public duty at this time. He managed to save the old Silbermann organ in the church of St. Thomas from being scrapped.

On the rainy day of May 13, 1908 Schweitzer, professor and medical student, presented himself for his first important medical examination. Only just before the decisive day did he consult the current list of usual questions and orthodox answers, and he went into the examination-room a tired man. But all turned out well.

Two days later this candidate in medicine entered the gynæcology clinic of the university as a demonstrator. At last he could devote his energies to real medical practice, and attend a birth. Normally Schweitzer was hardly inclined to nervousness, but that evening he was really upset. The longer the birth-pangs lasted the more restless he became, and there was a special reason for this. For next day at eleven o'clock he was to preach the wedding sermon at the church of St. Nicholas for his old friend Elly Knapp and her betrothed—a young author and politician named Theodor Heuss. Next day the bridal party and their guests were assembled at St. Nicholas. A boys'

choir had been mustered, Professor Knapp's university colleagues had arrived, clad in morning dress, the mayor himself
was present with the official marriage ceremony already completed. Elly Knapp's school-friends were there, Helene Bresslau among them, and Heuss had invited his chief, too, the fiery
orator and political radical, Friedrich Naumann. Only
Schweitzer was missing. On the stroke of eleven o'clock a
carriage came galloping up to the church, containing Albert
Schweitzer, still wearing his white medical jacket. Two
minutes later he stood in church, attired in his black Geneva
gown, ready to perform the ceremony. He always remembered the smell of carbolic soap as he preached.

Many years later the bride, then wife of the President of the
German Federal Republic, recalled one passage of Schweitzer's
sermon.

> The supreme inspiration of this moment does not lie in the
> fact that two persons have in their hearts vowed to live for each
> other but that in their minds such a vow implies that they will live
> with each other for something, in the service of some cause. . . .
> Only those have understood the great issues at stake in our times
> who have realized that all service, all attempts at amelioration and
> progress must lead to the creation of a new spirit.

Still his long struggle against sleep went on: there was the
study of pharmaceutics with Cahn and Schmiedeberg, of surgery with Madelung and Ledderhose, of bacteriology with
Forster and Levy. Between times there were journeys to Bayreuth for festivals, lectures on the Apostles, night-long discussions about the formulation of guiding principles for an international attempt at a Vienna congress to save the old art of
organ-building, and ever more and more concerts. The climax
was his participation in the Munich Festival of French art, on
which occasion Widor, who was late, had to conduct almost
half of one of his works without spectacles and escaped a
musical *débâcle* only through Schweitzer's rhythmically firm
organ-playing. Abdominal operations and oratorios, con-

With his daughter Rhena, 1928

The hospital village at Lambaréné. The operating room is on the left

firmation classes in his native village and champagne break-
fasts at the table of a wealthy admirer, and increasing piles of
letters which had to be answered.

Besides all this he was suffering from a private sorrow:
early in 1909 Helene Bresslau, after a summer holiday which
she spent visiting Russia, gave up her post as orphan guardian
in order to complete her training as a nurse at Frankfurt. For
the first time Schweitzer felt how much he missed her as a
silent, ever-helpful friend.

Just about this time there was a visiting student at the Strasbourg university clinic whose name was Frau Morel. She was
the wife of an Alsatian missionary, on leave in Europe. Since
1908 she and her husband had been working at the mission
station of Lambaréné on the Ogowe. They had been taking
university courses in order to extend and deepen their knowledge of medicine.

Albert Schweitzer was introduced to Frau Morel by the
head of the clinic, and at once began to ask questions. The next
day he brought a bag of pralines with him, slipped them into
her hand, and invited her to call on him.

Thus the next afternoon four people sat round the tea table
in Schweitzer's home on the St. Thomas Quayside: the two
Morels, Schweitzer, and Helene Bresslau (now back in Strasbourg). He had invited Helene ostensibly to play the part of
hostess, but no doubt his real purpose was somewhat different:
he wished to give her the opportunity of hearing for once from
eye-witnesses of the difficulties of life in the tropics.

At the close of the afternoon, Frau Morel reported later to a
friend, Schweitzer suddenly announced to the guests his engagement to Fräulein Bresslau. In view of Schweitzer's ex-
treme reserve about private and personal matters, it is very
probable that not only the Morels but also Helene herself heard
then for the first time of this happy resolve by the man who
was to be her future husband.

This sudden encounter with the future had a tragicomic ending. For in order to celebrate the engagement and learn still more about Africa, Helene Bresslau invited the two missionaries to visit her parents' home on the following afternoon. This time the questions came not from one, but from two: both Albert and Helene wanted to know so much, and the questions rattled down so sharply, that poor Frau Morel, as she used to relate afterwards with a laugh, fainted for the first and only time in her life. When she had recovered Albert Schweitzer took the whole party, at about ten o'clock that evening, to the church of St. Thomas, and played the organ to them.

In December 1911 Schweitzer was examined by the surgeon Madelung in the final stage of the complicated State medical examination system. He had earned his examination fees by his organ recitals.

> When I stepped out of the hospital into the darkness of the winter night I could hardly grasp the fact that the terribly strenuous exertions which my medical studies had demanded of me, were now over,

he writes in *My Life and Thought*.

> As if from a great distance I heard Madelung, who was walking beside me, say over and over again: "It is only because you enjoy excellent health that you have been able to bring off a thing like this."

Now it was a question of doing unpaid practical work for a further year in the clinics, writing a doctorate thesis, and above all taking leave of his friends. He must now say good-bye to the second lecture-room to the east of the main university entrance, where, as a theology professor, he had been accustomed to deliver his lectures, he must take leave, too, of his circle of musical friends in Strasbourg and Paris, and of the congregation of St. Nicholas.

The last Sunday afternoon sermon of the Reverend Doctor Schweitzer took place on February 25, 1912. The curate had chosen as his text a verse from the Revelation of St. John: "Be thou faithful unto death and I will give thee a crown of life."

"For the last time it is my privilege to preach to you in this church at a Sunday afternoon devotional service," he began. "These Sunday afternoon services have been for me among the most beautiful things that I have experienced in the whole course of my life. You have no doubt noticed that in recent years I have been able to perform my duty only with fatigue and by summoning my last reserves of strength, and many a time as I left the pulpit I have had the impression that you must have been very indulgent with me."

Many eyes were filled with tears, and many who up till now had blamed the pastor for his intention of leaving them and devoting his whole energies to sick negroes, realized at this moment that he could no other, if he were to remain true to himself and so faithful both to them and to his God.

All of them—student friends, teachers, acquaintances, and relations—had up to now still clung to the fond hope that he would reverse his decision. Now they realized they must let go such an illusion. The realization hit most harshly of all one human being who so far had not been mixed up in the conflict around Albert Schweitzer, but who had silently hoped that in the end he would change his mind: this was his mother. Now on a walk in the Altenbach Valley near Günsbach she sought to bring pressure to bear on her son and at the last moment to turn him from his purpose. Schweitzer listened quietly to what she had to say and then answered her by a single quotation: "Whosoever putteth his hand to the plough and looketh back is not worthy of the Kingdom of God."

She was never again to see her son after his departure from Europe.

CHAPTER 8

Setting out on a New Life

FOR A LONG time Schweitzer had been saving all the spare money which came to him from his work on Bach (now published in three languages), from recital fees, and from his theological writings towards the expenses of his African adventure. He now accepted the proposal of an American music publisher that in collaboration with his master Widor, he should prepare an edition of Bach's organ works, so that the advance payment in dollars should be added to his funds. But thousands of French francs were still wanted. For this reason Albert Schweitzer had to go on his rounds begging, to find patrons for his adventurous scheme.

Schweitzer's cause was made more difficult in the year 1912 because of the great tension between the German Empire and the Third French Republic. The setting up of a French protectorate over Morocco had only recently led to an acute crisis in the relations between Paris and Berlin. More than ever the talk now was of unavoidable war. Quarrelsome speeches east and west of the Rhine became ever louder and fiercer. Naturally the tension was especially painful in Strasbourg, where all intercourse and association between Francophiles and Germanophiles were broken off: Elly Heuss-Knapp, for example, could no longer be seen with her old friend Pierre Bucher, who published the *Alsatian Review*, noted for its Parisian tendencies.

It was at the height of this tense situation that Albert Schweitzer dared to beg money from the German middle-class and professional families on behalf of a charitable work which he was going to carry out in a French colony. But he begged from the French too. The Paris Bach Society organized a concert, all the takings of which were handed over to him, and in Le Havre two organizations raised a very considerable sum of money. The German professors of the University of Strasbourg gave generously for his plans; the members of the church of St. Nicholas turned out to be unusually lavish in their donations; pupils and friends of Schweitzer collected eagerly. "The affection which I encountered on these errands a hundred times outweighed the humiliations which I had to put up with," Schweitzer himself said, summing up his experiences of the spring of 1912.

Just as humiliating as some of his attempts to raise money must have been his first approaches to the leaders of the Paris Missionary Society. Far from receiving with open arms this voluntary helper who had made such costly personal sacrifices, certain members of the mission treated him as though he were an accused and dangerous man. This did not surprise Schweitzer at all. Already in 1905, when he first announced to Alfred Boegner, at that time the head of the society, his intention of serving as a doctor to the Congo mission, this friendly and warm-hearted man prepared him for such difficulties.

The Paris Missionary Society was controlled by pietistic circles of orthodox Protestant believers to whom Schweitzer's liberal Protestant outlook must have been abhorrent. His historical and critical examination of the legendary Christ of the Church and of theology had raised such a dust of controversy that the author must have seemed to many influential members a sheer heretic. Hence, when he called on Alfred Boegner's successor, the secretary Jean Bianquisy in the society's offices in the Boulevard Arago, the latter was pleased to hear the news that Schweitzer had himself raised enough money for the building of a small hospital in the Lambaréné mission station.

Schweitzer agreed to visit each of the committee members personally. Thus he would not have the feeling that they were sitting in collective judgment on him. He writes in *My Life and Thought*:

> Some few of them received me coldly. Most of them assured me that my theological standpoint caused them to hesitate, especially because I might be tempted to lead missionaries astray through my knowledge and desire to become active as a preacher myself. When I promised them that I only wanted to be a doctor and as for the rest intended to be "as dumb as a carp," they were satisfied. By these visits I even gained a really cordial relationship to a number of the members of this committee.

Only one member remained irreconcilable and even went so far as to resign. The others agreed, even though with hesitation. Some perhaps had realized from the robust, self-confident, and yet modest way in which the man presented himself that they were faced with some one of quite outstanding calibre.

Thus one further stage on the long road to Africa was passed. Schweitzer could now at last think of collecting drugs, instruments, bandaging material, provisions and some of the most necessary objects for the equipment of a hospital. Many hours had now to be spent in the offices and store-rooms of pharmaceutical establishments in order to compare prices and purchase the very best with the money available. For Schweitzer was of the opinion—and remained faithful to the principle in all subsequent years—that you must be more careful in the spending of money you have been given for some purpose than in the spending of your own resources. His quite fanatical economizing spirit, which by many of his collaborators was regarded as excessive, would not even allow him to throw away unused a sheet of paper, an old box, or even a bit of string.

In the midst of all these preparations, on June 18, 1912, Albert Schweitzer married Helene Bresslau. It is entirely characteristic that in *My Life and Thought* he mentions the fact in an interpolated clause as though it were of quite subsidiary importance. And indeed in all this rush of activity the ceremonial side of the occasion was severely reduced. In the circum-

stances a honeymoon was not to be thought of. When at last
they were alone Albert and Helene were to be found bent over
the correcting of his doctorate thesis, which was concerned
with the interpretation of Jesus as a psychiatrist, and over the
printed proofs of an additional chapter for a new edition of his
work on the historical Jesus.

Albert Schweitzer was thirty-eight years old when, on the
afternoon of Good Friday, 1913, he started for Africa. He was
already fully aware of the difficulties that would face him
there. From the courses in tropical medicine which he had
attended in Paris before his departure he knew only too well
the terrible diseases of tropical Africa. He realized how vicious
the climate could be, how the white man was soon overcome
and undermined by a fearful lassitude which either compelled
him to flee or else laid him low.

Nevertheless it must be. The church bells of Günsbach were
ringing. The Good Friday service had just ended. Pastor
Louis Schweitzer, as he did every year on this supremely holy
day, had related and tried to explain to his congregation the
climax of the Passion of Christ. Now he stood with his family
on the small railway station platform in order to bid good-bye
to his eldest son.

"In two years they will be here again," was the remark with
which one of the sisters comforted herself and her parents,
while Albert and Helene waved from the last carriage of the
train which disappeared behind the edge of the forest. Every
twenty-four months the missionary doctor intended to come
home to Günsbach for a few months on leave in order to renew his strength for the next period in Africa. But even in this
respect he cherished few illusions, for on his chest he wore a
purse containing two thousand marks in gold—in case of war.

In fact, the shadow of war lay over France and Germany.
Uniforms were to be seen everywhere, and war materials were
being loaded on trucks in railway sidings. The sight of this
spoiled the two travellers' pleasure in the dream-like beauty of
the journey across France, where warm spring breezes were

71

heavy with the clangour of church bells and the fragrance of spring blossom.

But on their arrival in Bordeaux on Easter Monday the Schweitzers were struck by an example of the helpfulness of individual goodwill in the face of harsh official regulations. Strictly speaking, the customs officer should not have examined their heavy luggage, which had been sent on in advance, until Easter Tuesday. But that would probably have meant that they would not have been able to reach the ship. When this difficulty was explained, there was a smile, a shrug of the shoulders suggesting that after all one is a human being and not an automatic jumping jack.

With all their trunks and boxes the Schweitzers arrived in good time at the dock where the ship was moored. It was the *Europe*—a warning reminder of the home continent which they were leaving. What was its real business? And what and whom was it taking to Africa? Schweitzer scanned the faces of the many strangers when the company was assembled for the first time in the dining-room of the ship. What will these people be doing in two to three years' time? he asked himself.

Shy as the new chickens which Schweitzer's mother put in the pen every summer among the old cocks and hens, the two new-comers sat at the table alongside experienced African travellers. They ate their meal in silence, and tried to infer from the expression on their neighbours' faces, from their gestures and from scattered shreds of conversation, the answer to that haunting question which filled their minds with disquieting tension: What is it really like in Africa?

In the early days of their voyage the Schweitzers did not learn very much on this score. Their ship, which was built with a shallow draught so that it might also be a river-boat for some distance up the Congo, began to roll heavily as soon as the open sea was reached. But after Teneriffe the weather improved. Flying fish danced round the boat, which was now passing through calm waters, gleaming in the sun. But this sun was no friend. The doctor remembered now the promise which he had made years before to an old friend of his in Strasbourg—the Countess of Erlach—that he would never go out in the tropics without some sort of head covering. When that evening Albert and Helene took out their white tropical clothes and helmets, still very fresh and redolent of the factory, they must have felt somewhat like recruits putting on uniform for the first time, or still more like novices exchanging their worldly garments for the conventual habit.

At Dakar they entered the harbour, and were brought to land in a long-boat, and now at last their feet touched that other continent—the continent of Africa—the land of the negro!

And then they were plunged into it. A heavily laden cart had got stuck on a newly macadamized road. The lean, wretched-looking beast could not pull his load any farther. The two drivers were lashing out at it with the whip, and screaming curses.

Schweitzer was soon beside the cart, forcing the two native drivers to get down from their seat. The three men pushed the cart out on to another section of the road. The negroes had not a word of thanks for their helper—a white man—who stood there stroking the little beast on its thin neck. The horse did not even look up. It was far too tired and stupefied.

The Schweitzers' companion, a colonial lieutenant whom they had got to know on board, stood watching the scene from the roadside, shaking his head.

"If you can't endure to see animals ill-treated, don't come to Africa," he said. "You will see plenty of that kind of horror here."

CHAPTER 9

Africa's Lessons

PEPPER COAST, Ivory Coast, Gold Coast, Slave Coast . . . the *Europe* rolled along by the shores of West Africa. Albert and Helene Schweitzer, leaning over the ship's rail, peered out at the thickly wooded strips of land, over which violent storms burst from time to time.

A fellow passenger, employed by a large firm, returning for the third time to his work on the Congo, commented to Schweitzer:

"We westerners take the negro brandy and gin and various diseases which he did not previously know. Do the blessings we bring really outweigh the evils that go with them?"

It was a question on which Schweitzer often meditated as the ship skirted the African coast.

The doctor and his wife must have felt it to be a striking confirmation of the ship's gossip about negroes when they saw the attitude of the fifty negroes on the poop who had been taken on board at Tabou as a loading crew. They were sturdy, capable fellows, proud of their muscles under their smooth, almost pitch-black skin, and of their physical adroitness. But how brutally they behaved towards other coloured men on board, whether servants or passengers! How different the cruelly arrogant expression in their eyes was from the meek countenance of that melancholy negro on the Colmar monument by which Schweitzer had been so deeply moved!

So much the greater was his joy when he met the negroes of the Baraka missionary station in Libreville, the last port of call before their arrival at Cape Lopez. The very name of this Christian outpost was reminiscent of the horrors of the slave

74

trade, for Portuguese traders named their big slave camps "barakons". Schweitzer was impressed by the cleanliness of the people, their friendly smiling faces, so unlike those of the men of Tabou or the sullen dejected negroes he had seen in their other ports of call.

The fear of the colonial Customs at Cape Lopez, which they had long entertained, and which had been intensified by the gloomy prophecies of their fellow passengers, turned out to have been excessive. With anxious faces the Schweitzers produced the painfully exact and clear list of the contents of their seventy trunks. This very correct procedure pleased the officials and the business was quickly despatched. One last night on the ship, during which there roared around them the noise of the loading of cranes, the cries of dockyard workers, the din of coals bumping about in the hold, and then it was really "*Adieu, Europe.*"

The river-steamer *Alembe* lay unloading in the primitive roadstead. It was now taking on board only passengers and their hand luggage; the big freight was sent on separately. Black men with huge bundles climbed on board, and squatted in the lower part of the ship, while in the upper part were the white people's cabins. Not all of those due to travel had arrived on time. But it was impossible to wait for them any longer, since the tide which was to carry the *Alembe* safely over the sandbanks at the entrance of the Ogowe was now at its height.

The dark-skinned pilot steered his way into one of the many arms of the river. He knew his course well enough despite the many pitfalls. But he had to be constantly on the watch, for the sluggish stream carried huge scattered tree-trunks down to the sea on its broad, dirty, yellowish back, which made the waterway dangerous. Fragments of the ribs of wooden rafts were borne to the ocean from the heart of the continent. It was not worth while to pick them up, for the wood was already far too rotten. But the logs almost made boats capsize, endangered the paddle-wheels of river-steamers, and in the darkness frightened many people, who took them for the backs of crocodiles or hippopotamuses.

Faced by this immense, ancient landscape of river and forest, everything that had ever happened to Schweitzer seemed to recede. He followed the heavy flight of a heron, and watched two small monkeys on the crest of a palm-tree. Was it for an hour? Two hours? Or only a minute? The same images confronted him, the same rotting stump, the ponderous river bird, the same gliding yellowish waters, branching off into multiple streams, weaving their way round little islands, forming lakes and lazy curves, opening up new vistas—the same eternal forest, the same sluggish waves.

"When I came to this country fifteen years ago," a trader observed to Schweitzer, "there were flourishing villages here."

"Why are they so no longer?"

"Alcohol . . . most of the money earned through the wood trade is squandered on rum. I have knocked around in the colonies of various nations. Rum is the enemy of all attempts at civilized life."

The boat called at a village to take in fuel. Wooden logs were lying piled up near the mooring-place. The captain scolded the village chief.

"You have not enough logs ready here." A long wordy palaver began, with much gesticulation and shouting.

"That's typical," said the trader. "The black man would rather be paid in rum than in money. He thinks that we white men get the alcohol tax free, and that thus he will be better off."

The village receded into the gathering darkness, and

> With the deepening dusk of the first night on the Ogowe there lowers over one the shadow of the misery of Africa, [Schweitzer later confessed]. . . . And I feel more convinced than ever that this land needs to help it men who will never let themselves be discouraged.

The next day Albert Schweitzer reached that other pole of his world and his second home: Lambaréné. After a night in a backwater of the river, the steamer paddled on its way. Two hours were spent at the mission station of N'Gomo in order to load enough logs for the ship's boiler once more. The doctor and his wife were now all impatience: in another five hours they would be at their destination.

To the accompaniment of blasts on the steamer's siren—how often was Schweitzer to hear it again in the course of the next forty years—they approached Lambaréné. The signals were given a full half-hour before docking so that officials at the trading settlements, the postal authorities, and the missionaries would be prepared in good time. The journey from the landing-stage to the Lambaréné mission on a tributary of the Ogowe was made in a canoe.

The canoe was a hollowed-out tree-trunk, and the rowers stood in it holding their long narrow paddles. The crew struck the water rhythmically, singing as they paddled. The Schweitzers sat rather fearfully in the canoe, afraid to move in case they upset it.

Upstream the canoe raced the steamer and then turned into a branch of the stream where in the light of the setting sun the Schweitzers saw the houses of the mission station on a rising hill. The singing grew louder, and then quite suddenly the canoe glided into a quiet little bay.

A hearty welcome awaited them at the mission station.

The doctor and his wife were still sitting on their cases in their new house listening to a welcoming chorale whose harmonies rang out from the schoolroom, when suddenly Helene uttered a gentle cry. Schweitzer looked up. In the light of the oil lamp he saw an uncanny shadow on the wall: a colossal spider was just about to pounce on his wife's head.

"An exciting hunt, and the creature is done for," was Schweitzer's account of his first spider chase.

After supper by the light of Chinese lanterns the doctor and his wife were led back to their house, where the battle against

the spiders and cockroaches began. Waving a big handker-
chief, Schweitzer tried to drive them away. Attracted by the
light, the creatures swarmed and whirled through the door,
which, with their lack of experience in Africa, the visitors were
unable to keep sealed, and also through holes in the wiring
which spanned the window of the house, which had stood
empty for so long.

It was their first night on African soil. Their first day began
at six o'clock next morning.

CHAPTER 10

Only Four Hands

THE HANDS OF the organist, trained to command the finest differences of touch on the keyboards, were now handling spars, hammers, and paint-brushes. The hands of the one-time student of the history of art were now washing, cleaning, cutting, and scrubbing.

How many things a tropical doctor has to think of who has no well-equipped hospital prepared for his use! Where is he to find materials suitable for building? Where is he to get the builders from? Where is he to get his water? How is he to clear away rubbish and dirt and infectious waste? And how many troubles Nature puts in his way—sand fleas and stinging insects, rats and mosquitoes, whole armies of warring ants who march in disciplined formation and then swarm out to assault human beings, biting their way into the skin.

The news soon spread through the jungle that a new doctor had come to Lambaréné, a new clever medicine man with charms and fetishes. Meanwhile the Schweitzers had not even enough bandaging materials, ointments, and potions to treat their nearest neighbours. "Come back in three weeks' time," was the doctor's daily advice to his first would-be patients.

About the end of the month the boxes with the most-needed things arrived at last from Cape Lopez. For three days the mission school-children, under the supervision of their teacher, the doctor, and his wife, dealt with the despatch of the new luggage upstream from the landing-place to the mission. Even then everything had to be dragged up the steep hill to Schweitzer's house, where medicines were arranged on shelves fixed up around the walls of the living-room.

The doctor started his African career in the open air under the leaden sky of the tropics, for there was no hospital, not even one room to use. Patients were carried up the hill and laid on the ground. Schweitzer walked from one to the other, examining festering wounds, and binding up old injuries. And then, suddenly, heavy drops of rain would begin to fall. The daily storm had begun. Amid the rumbling of thunder the doctor and his wife and an assistant hastily moved the bottles, the bandages, the rugs, and the instruments on to the veranda of the house. The patients were soon borne away by their relatives to the shelter of a hut. Five minutes later the sun would be out again and burning fiercely. Once again a tent was erected under the open sky, and the space before the house again became a thronging mass of sick folk.

"Practising in the sun was overwhelmingly tiring," Dr. Schweitzer confessed a few weeks later in a letter to a friend at home. It was the sun that drove him to the shelter of a disused hen-house for his first dispensary. The place was scrubbed through and cleaned with soap and broom. Then the walls were whitewashed and the floor disinfected. The missionary carpenter Kast soon fixed up shelves of the finest mahogany and ebony, which was more easily obtainable there than ordinary deal. An old plank bed was transformed into a table, and the jungle doctor, now established in quite a distinguished fashion, could contentedly hang up his doctor's plate in front of the door.

"There are no heroes of action, only heroes of renunciation and suffering," is a thought that occurs in one of Schweitzer's writings. In spite of all his modesty he may justly rank himself among those heroes. During just those first months at Lambaréné he and his wife learned to do without. Their friends, the stimulus and joy of artistic experience, their comforts, which were of the most modest and unpretentious kind— all these European amenities were now gladly renounced. They were also prepared to forget the sweetness of drinking

At the organ: Europe and Africa

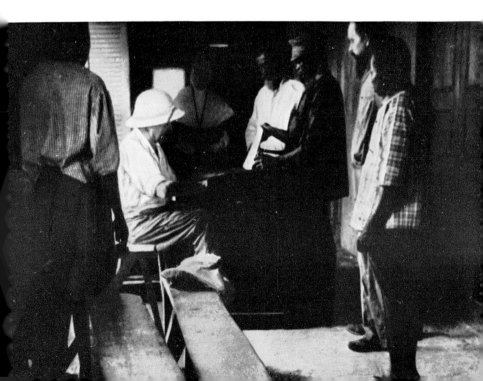

Schweitzer receives an honorary degree at Chicago University, 1949

fresh cold water. Nor did they complain of the monotonous jungle food, which they ate without their accustomed vegetables, salads, and fruit. All this they had fully expected and they were ready and eager to adapt themselves to this new life at Lambaréné.

Schweitzer's consultation time began at half-past eight in the morning. His two assistants, of whom one was a former cook named Joseph, and the other the teacher N'Zeng, would arrange patients on the benches in the shade of the former henhouse.

Then one of them would read out the standing orders from the doctor, freely translated into the Goloa dialect, while the other repeated them in the Pahouin dialect. They went like this:

> You are not to spit so that your worms do not attack other sick folk.
>
> The white doctor needs quiet when he is cheating the illness. If you speak too loudly he cannot slay it unnoticed.
>
> Bring enough to eat with you for the whole day. Many will have to wait until the sun goes down.
>
> Not all of you can remain here overnight.
>
> Bring back your bottles and tin boxes when the medicine is finished.
>
> In the middle of the month only those who are very seriously ill must come to the doctor. During that time he writes for the healing medicines to the land of the white men.
>
> Tell everyone you meet what you have just heard.

The patients would nod their heads as though they understood and accepted these terms. Then, however, they would begin to spit, and to chatter noisily with each other; they stole food from the mission plantations, they crept at night into the dormitories of the mission school and simply threw the pupils out of bed; they lost and embezzled their medicine bottles, or left them lying about in the mission grounds; they besieged the doctor's house around the middle of the month in greater numbers than ever, and never thought of telling others about the doctor's orders.

It was not easy for Albert Schweitzer to keep his patience, and still more difficult was it to continue to show towards these troublesome patients that over-riding sympathy and self-sacrificial charity which was the driving force behind this daily giving of strength, health, and time.

The worst thing of all was that so many of these sick people simply would not do what the doctor told them. They fumbled about with recent operation wounds, and ignored the diet rules. When they were only half healed they went to bathe in the dirty river, or vanished before the treatment was complete.

One day when Joseph told the doctor that a man had gone back to his tribe, taking with him his child who was still seriously ill, just because he had some quite insignificant dispute to settle there, Schweitzer got angry and shouted:

"What a fool I was to come out here to you savages!"

"Yes," answered his assistant, "you are a fool in the eyes of men, but not in the eyes of God."

Joseph became, with Helene, the most indispensable of the doctor's helpers. Of course he was vain and fond of dress, like most others. He complained constantly of his salary, which seemed to him too small. Did he not formerly earn more in Cape Lopez than in his present sphere, where in his opinion he had become an intellectual? He spent about half of his wages on ties, perfume, bad patent-leather shoes, and similar goods which were shipped out from France.

And yet, when Joseph, as the doctor's first assistant, was doing his job in the stifling fowl-house, he showed real efficiency. In the confined space there was hardly enough room for three people, and yet the work went booming on. The doctor saw from thirty to forty patients a day.

"Where is your pain?" he would ask through an interpreter.

"An evil spirit is gnawing at me," a woman would point to her breast.

Schweitzer examined her, putting the stethoscope to her heart.

"You must be sleeping badly at nights. You have difficulties in breathing. Your feet are swollen."

"Yes, that is true. But how do you know, doctor, what the evil spirit is doing to me? You must possess great power."

"Here are some drops. Take ten every day in a little water. Repeat how you are to take the medicine."

"Ten every day in a little water."

"Joseph, take her out and make her repeat it ten times. And give her the necklace."

The necklace was a bit of bast string, on which hung a small cardboard disc. On the disc were the number, name, illness, and the remedy which each patient received. Thus each was readily distinguishable next time from other patients, and his pathological record could easily be looked up in the big book.

Unfortunately the patients were unable to read how the medicine given them was to be taken. From forgetfulness, or because they thought they knew better, they would drink the whole bottle straight off instead of a few drops at a time, or they would rub a stomach powder into the skin of their stomach, and gulp down a healing ointment.

Schweitzer's local fame was made by a healing ointment which he invented himself to cure scabies. Whole families came flocking to him. They camped everywhere in the mission grounds; they cooked their food and quarrelled loudly.

The doctor wrote home:

But what are these temporary difficulties compared with the joy of being able to work out here and render service? However limited the resources much can still be done with them. Merely to see the joy of those burdened with ulcers when at last their wounds are wholesomely bound up and they need no longer run about in dirt with their sore feet, makes it amply worth while to work here. (From *On the Edge of the Primeval Forest*.)

Soon the fame enjoyed by the new doctor was so great that the natives began to compare him with Eliwa N'Guewa. This coloured dancer was a mysterious legendary figure. It was said of her that she could dance on the water without sinking. All the big water-lilies bloomed when the beautiful Eliwa came near them, while all the evil spirits fled from their dwellings in rotted trees, decaying huts, and the bodies of the sick and wicked. That was a paradisal time on the Ogowe. Would it come again now that the great doctor was working at the Lambaréné mission?

Songs about the dancer's magical beauty and her gentle but irresistible power were sung on journeys by boat, when the oarsmen would burst forth into new lyrical strains about spirits and monsters, about themselves and their passengers.

On one occasion Schweitzer, accompanied by the two missionaries Christol and Ellenberger, had himself rowed upstream to Samkita. Twelve bare, muscular men worked their paddles with unbroken rhythm. "Oh, what a hot sultry day is coming," they sang, "so early the dawn, so late the sunset."

It was Albert Schweitzer's first river journey since he had set foot in Lambaréné. Even now, after three months of hard work, he would scarcely have been willing to undertake it had it not been for the sake of his patients. At Samkita, where the Protestant missionaries in that part of Africa gathered together once a year, he was to make a plea for the building of his hospital, which could no longer be put off.

What a glorious river trip! Tufted cranes fluttered and soared, kingfishers circled round them with outstretched wings, giant butterflies in fantastic glittering colours hovered against the sombre masses of jungle overshadowing the banks. But still more glorious was the plumage of the pipilo. It shimmered green-gold and sparkled with myriads of gem-like facets.

Schweitzer went to Samkita with very mixed feelings. He was afraid that the resident established missionaries might reveal themselves to be as narrow and petty as some of the directors of the mission in Paris. But he found here among these active missionaries a breadth of outlook, a generosity, and a courageous spirit of self-sacrifice which were an inspiration to him, refreshing and warming his heart.

The missionaries were warm in their approval of him. They were pleasantly surprised to discover that the theologian, philosopher, and doctor was himself prepared to design and build the hospital. They gladly granted him the proposed site, and furthermore they had some unexpectedly good news for him. For at the close of the discussion they voted four thousand francs for the new Lambaréné hospital.

First of all the new building site had to be levelled. With great difficulty five Africans were procured to undertake this enormously strenuous job. But, as Schweitzer reported to his wife one evening, "their finest success consisted in laziness". At this point help came from an unexpected quarter. A timber trader named Rapp who was among Schweitzer's acquaintances happened to be staying in the neighbourhood. He placed eight carriers at the doctor's disposal. "I promised them handsome pay," Schweitzer wrote, "and took a spade in hand myself, while the black foreman lay in the shade of a tree and occasionally threw us an encouraging word."

The ground was levelled within two days.

"I know," the doctor said, "that there are too few of us to manage all the work. We really have only four reliable hands, and it is not enough. But soon other hands will be forthcoming to help us. I know that for certain."

That evening, for the first time, he opened the tropical piano sheathed in tin casing which the Paris Society had given him. In the disorderly chaos of the jungle emerged the clear luminous sounds of the structure of a Bach fugue. The hands of Albert Schweitzer, musician and builder, had not lost their skill.

CHAPTER 11

Forest Doctor

WHEN THE HOSPITAL building was finished, it consisted of
two large rooms: the surgery and the operating theatre. It
had also two smaller rooms which were used for the dispensing
of medicines and for the purposes of sterilization. Next door
was a waiting-room, and spacious wards for the seriously ill.
A special hut had been built for Joseph, as medical assistant.
Such was the nucleus of the hospital village of Lambaréné. It
had its own landing-place shaded by a huge mango-tree, where
the patients could tie up their canoes.

In the wards, the floors were of firmly pounded clay, and the
beds were made of four simple posts on which sticks were
arranged lengthwise and crosswise, tightly bound together by
liana. There was no bed-linen. The mattresses were of cloth
and dried grass. These beds, however, were wide enough to
accommodate not only the patient but usually two of the
friends who came with him. If a lot of relations came as escorts,
then they camped on the floor near the bed. (It sometimes
happened that the relations left the sick men to lie on the floor,
while they themselves used the more comfortable bed.)
Schweitzer allowed men and women to sleep in the same ward,
and he also allowed the family to cook for themselves and their
sick relative in the grounds of the hospital.

It was a quite instinctive principle of Schweitzer's to adapt
his hospital as far as possible to the surroundings his patients
were used to, so that they might feel at home. This no doubt
caused much head-shaking among the official government
doctors of the district. But the missionary doctor was justified
by results. Whereas the Africans normally avoided attendance

at the white doctors' clinics, or attended only with the greatest
reluctance, the "Oganga of Lambaréné" was unable to escape
from the ever-increasing stream of patients.

In the first nine months at Lambaréné Schweitzer calculated
that he examined and treated about 2,000 patients. A strangulated hernia was a common occurrence, causing the sufferer
very severe pain. Such a case had to be operated on at once.

While his wife and Joseph made the final preparations for
the operation, Schweitzer went up to the agonized patient,
laid his cooling hand on the man's forehead, and comforted
him with the words, "Be calm. Very soon you will be asleep.
And when you wake up you will have no more pain."

His wife went to the patient, who had already been quietened
by an injection, and put the chloroform mask on his face. She
watched the pulse and observed the progress of the anæsthetic.
Joseph had put on the rubber gloves and stood by to assist.

The operation was a complicated one, and had to be finished
by lamplight. Later the doctor went to the patient's sleeping
quarters and waited for him to wake. As the man opened his
eyes he whispered, "I have no more pain. I have no more pain!"
In feverish gratitude he groped for the doctor's hand and
held it.

Then the doctor began to tell him and the other patients that
the Lord Jesus had bidden him and his wife come out to help
sick Africans.

"Why are there men in Europe who give money so that
you can come out here and help us?" someone asked.

"How do such people know that there are so many sick
people among us?" came another question. "What do they
get out of helping us?"

"We are all brothers," said the doctor. "So Jesus Christ my
God has declared."

"I have no more pain," murmured the rescued man again
in a tone of bewildered astonishment. And as he fell asleep,
Schweitzer wished that the friends who had given him money
could be there to see.

Schweitzer was at one and the same time surgeon, dentist, and children's doctor. He treated catarrh and diarrhœa, malaria and ulcers. Even Joseph, who knew how to watch with the closest attention, had already learnt to diagnose and prescribe for simple cases.

Mixing the terminology of his old and new professions, the ex-cook would announce proudly to his master: "I have myself bathed and bound up wounds on the woman's right joint," or, after his preliminary examination, "He has a pain in the upper left cutlet."

It was fortunate that Joseph became so independent and reliable, for the doctor operated at least three times a week, and sometimes he spent a whole morning over a blood test, because a patient was suspected of being afflicted with sleeping sickness.

Schweitzer gave particular attention to sleeping sickness for the special reason that as a white man he felt himself in part responsible for the spread of the disease. Originally it was confined to a few specific centres of infection, but as the restless white races roamed across the portion of the earth inhabited by coloured people, the dangerous microbe living in the blood and spinal marrow of an infected person was carried to other regions. Then it was spread by the tsetse fly, and could, in Schweitzer's early days, decimate whole tribes and depopulate whole villages. In the Ogowe area there had been no sleeping sickness until 1880, when it was brought in by the porters of an expedition coming from the Loango district.

Most gruesome was the sight of afflicted people in the later stages of the disease, staggering around in broad daylight like sleep-walkers, and finally stumbling on to the ground with no power to raise themselves, lying unconscious on the bare earth, thin as skeletons, covered with sores, and with carrion flies crawling all over them.

When the disease had progressed thus far, Schweitzer could be of little use. The germs had bored their way from the bloodstream into the fluid marrow of brain and back, with inflammation of the cerebral membranes, resulting in inevitable painful death.

How much vain effort was he burdened with in the struggle against sleeping sickness! Every patient who merely complained of pains in the head or rheumatism was suspected of the disease. His blood had to be patiently investigated, and only when several drops of blood had been examined under the microscope was there a chance of discovering the malignant parasite. A tiny pale speck only the 18,000th part of a milli-metre in size had to be found, and this type of investigation, lasting for at least an hour, was not always reliable.

Often, of course, all the recognized methods of diagnosis failed to establish the nature of an illness. In spite of the most careful nursing, some patients languished and died. What had happened to them? Was it blood-poisoning? Joseph maintained that many of the patients who came to Lambaréné in those days had been poisoned. At first Schweitzer simply refused to believe it. Certainly there were strange poisonous plants unknown in Europe, with which the forest people stained the tips of their arrows. There were medicine men, magicians, and avengers, who, it was said, preferred to use very slow-working poisons mixed in food. But Schweitzer was inclined to place these stories among the ancient legends of the primeval forest.

He was confronted, however, by a medical riddle when an elderly man was brought to him, who, according to the statements of his fellow tribesmen, had become a raving maniac. The lianas cut deep into his flesh, his hands and feet were covered with blood, and he was full of self-inflicted wounds.

Schweitzer diagnosed a state of maniacal excitement, and prescribed morphia. But the old man failed to show the normal reaction to it. It was as if he had been given no more than a mild solution of sugared water. The drug scopolamine was tried, and the result was almost nil. Instead of becoming drowsy the poor fellow tried to fling himself about more fiercely than ever. Injections of chloral hydrate and bromide of potassium were equally useless.

Joseph declared that the man was mad because he had been poisoned. There was nothing to be done with such people. He would get continually weaker and wilder, and finally he would collapse and die. Within fourteen days the man did die, probably poisoned from motives of revenge.

From then on Schweitzer kept his eyes open for such inexplicable cases. If a sick person did not show normal reactions to treatment there was always the suspicion that his friends who accompanied him and pretended to be his helpers and cooks were mixing poison with his food. Joseph then prepared the black potion.

The black potion was nothing other than charcoal and water intended to wash out and disinfect the stomach of the poisoned man. At the same time the patient's friends were tactfully given to understand that for a certain time he must be fed only by the hospital assistants.

One day Schweitzer witnessed a curious scene at the bedside of a dying patient. An African who had been seriously injured by a hippopotamus while fishing was operated on too late. After the operation the already dying man was lying on his bed in the ward. The doctor's wife was trying to soothe his pain by injections. When the poor fellow was at his last gasp his two escorts at the bedside began to quarrel, first in whispers, and then more and more loudly. Schweitzer grew angry at this insensitivity in the face of death. But Joseph took him aside in order to explain.

"The brother of the dead man is right in his accusations. The other fellow named N'Kendju is responsible for the accident. It was he who proposed going fishing where there are hippopotamuses, so the death lies at his door. He insists that N'Kendju shall go straight back with him to the village to answer for his crime, and the man refuses, for it means death."

Schweitzer's answer to that threat was to give N'Kendju a

job in the hospital, where he became a faithful servant to the doctor and his wife.

Such experiences were even more taxing to the strength and courage of Albert and Helene Schweitzer than the climate and the thousands of small annoyances that life in Equatorial Africa involves.

They began slowly to understand something of the hell of fear the forest people lived in. They were constantly in terror of the curse of powerful enemies or before the power of some native magician. Even the children learned early that life lay under the shadow of special taboos. One taboo was that a knock on the shoulder was sufficient to make the child fall dead. Another taboo warned against eating bananas. A mere bite and the child would writhe in death-convulsions. A pregnant woman, warned against the birth of a boy, behaved as if the baby was a girl. She called him by a girl's name, dressed him like a girl, and all her neighbours fell in with the ruse. Another mother, burdened by the taboo that if she gave birth to a girl she would die, refused to believe that by good luck she had brought forth a boy. She supposed that they were lying to her, and actually perished from her obsessive delusions. Thus powerful and terrible psychic forces were brought into action by the haunting dread which superstitions arouse; even the belief in the imminence of disaster could cause death.

At first Schweitzer thought it was merely laziness when some of the Africans implored him not to compel them to take part in the burial of the dead. Later he began to see that some taboo forbade them to do this and that he was wrongly condemning them without understanding their reasons.

But the most uncanny and oppressive thing of all were many murders committed in the forests of the Ogowe during Schweitzer's early years there purely from motives of superstition. If anybody desired to attain some particular object, the native magicians would usually advise the obtaining of a powerful fetish. Fetishes often included, besides feathers, fragments of plants, birds' claws, and other similar objects, pieces of the human skull. Sometimes the magician even required that this indispensable object should come from a near relative of the petitioner—a mother or father. In such circumstances sons would kill their parents solely to acquire a good fetish.

Helene Schweitzer was deeply shaken by such incidents. Often she felt it incomprehensible and unbelievable that the forest peoples should live under the shadow of such brutal laws, and that they should apparently know so little of love, goodness, and gratitude.

Schweitzer himself often looked round at his little group of hospital buildings where no taboo or magic or curse could prevail. But he also knew that away in Europe even civilized peoples believed in very strange fetishes, for example bits of coloured cloth which they called flags. The mere word of a chieftain in Moscow or Berlin, in Paris or London, could at any moment transform so-called cultured nations into head-hunters who required not merely a single fragment of the human skull to dispel their fear and to win their good fortune, but the sacrifice of millions of young lives.

It was the beginning of July 1914.

CHAPTER 12

Light in the Darkness

IN EUROPE SCHWEITZER had often been told that Christianity was too exalted a religion for the primitive peoples of Africa, and he had been deeply disquieted by this argument. But at Lambaréné he realized that the religion of love can not only be made comprehensible to primitive peoples, but also can bring them effective help in the keenest distresses of their souls.

To express this message Albert Schweitzer began once again to exercise his calling as a minister of religion at some of the Sunday services of the mission. His missionary colleagues released him from the promise to be "as mute as a carp" which the leaders of the mission had exacted from him at the outset of his venture. Nor had they any reason to regret their decision. The new preacher, taking into account the habits of mind and customary experiences of the natives, struck just the right note. When Schweitzer expounded the parables of Jesus, the Sermon on the Mount, and some of the teaching of the Apostle Paul, his words brought a new freedom of spirit.

He never preached a sermon without speaking against the delusion that the wielders of fetishes and magicians were in possession of a secret source of power. He knew that his African friends believed that he too was a magician, and were therefore the more deeply impressed when he plainly told them:

> I possess no other power than that of the knowledge which I have acquired and am now putting to use. I have dedicated these attainments to the service of God who loves all mankind, pardons, helps, and brings peace to the hearts of His children.

93

Had Albert Schweitzer expounded to his hearers the Ten Commandments, they simply would not have understood most of them. Lying, stealing, and immorality as understood by the Christian would certainly not have struck them as anything reprehensible, but rather as utterly natural and self-explanatory. In spite of all that, the former curate of St. Nicholas did not by any means consider his flock to be "bad". How often he was touched by their spontaneous goodness!

Whenever the doctor proposed to speak in the church, he always sat down in conference with his friend the African missionary teacher Ojembo in order to run through his sermon with him. For Ojembo was his translator, and after each of Schweitzer's sentences he gave an interpretation.

Most of all Schweitzer liked to speak in those early Lambaréné days about the peace of God, which dissolves strife within man's heart. Since his hearers were all constantly becoming entangled in some quarrel or other, the preacher hoped to be understood when he spoke, for example, about the necessity of forgiveness. He knew how to preach with unsurpassed cogency on the question addressed by Peter to Jesus whether it is enough to forgive seven times. He did so with mental pictures drawn from the world of his hearers' experience. The sermon then developed on the following lines:

> Hardly are you up in the morning and standing before your hut, when some one comes along who is detested by all as a wicked man and insults you. Because the Lord Jesus says that you are to forgive you prefer to be silent rather than begin a quarrel.
>
> Later your neighbour's goat eats the bananas which were to provide your midday meal. Instead of starting an argument with the neighbour you simply tell him that it was his goat and that it would be just for him to replace the bananas. But if he then contradicts you and maintains that it was not his goat you go away in silence and recollect that the dear God enables you to grow so many bananas in your plantation that there is no need to make a quarrel about those few. Shortly afterwards the man comes along to whom you gave ten bunches of

bananas that he might sell them for you in the market along with his own and brings you the money for nine only. You tell him that it is not enough. He however replies that you counted them wrongly and in fact only gave him nine bunches. At once you want to scream in his face that he is a liar. But then you must remember how many lies, which you alone know about, the dear God must forgive you, and you go back silently into your hut.

Then when you go to make your fire you become aware that somebody has stolen the wood which you gathered yesterday out of the forest, and which was to suffice for a week's cooking. Once again you compel your heart to forgive and restrain yourself from going and rummaging about in your neighbours' stocks to see who might have your wood and denouncing the thief to the chief justice.

In the afternoon when you start work in the plantation you discover that somebody has taken your fine bush knife and substituted for it his old and notched one. You know who it is for you recognise the knife. Then it occurs to you that you have forgiven four times and that you want to bring it off a fifth time. Although it is a day on which you have had a great deal of trouble you feel as happy as if it were one of your most successful days. Why? Because your heart is glad that it has been obedient to the will of the Lord Jesus.

In the evening you want to go fishing. You reach for the torch, which should be in the corner of the hut. But it isn't there. Then a wave of anger sweeps over you and you think that you have forgiven enough for to-day and that you will lie in wait for the man who went fishing with your torch. But once again the Lord Jesus masters your heart. You go down to the riverside with a torch which a neighbour has lent you.

There you discover that your boat is not there. Somebody else has gone fishing in it. Angrily you hide behind a tree in order to watch for the man who has played this trick on you and propose that on his return you will seize all his fish and accuse him before the chief officer of the district so that he pays you compensation as is just and right. But while you are waiting your heart begins to speak to you. Over and over again it reminds you of the words of the Lord Jesus who said that God cannot forgive us our trespasses unless we forgive our fellow creatures. You have to wait so long that the Lord Jesus once more masters your feelings. Instead of attacking the other fellow with your fists when at last he returns in the grey dawn, and starts back afraid when you emerge from behind the trees, you tell him that the Lord Jesus constrains you to forgive him and lets him go in peace. You do not even require him to hand over the fish, you take them only if he freely surrenders them. But I think he will give them to you if only from sheer astonishment that you do not start a quarrel with him.

Now you go home proud and happy to think that you have controlled yourself so as to forgive seven times. But if on that day the Lord Jesus were to come to your village and you went up to Him expecting that He would praise you before all on this account, then He would say to you as He did to Peter that seven times is not enough and that you must forgive seven times more and more and more and so on endlessly until God can forgive you your many sins. . . .

It is a curious paradox that just in those months and weeks which preceded the outbreak of the First World War, Schweitzer in remotest Africa preached with passionate emphasis about the Christian principles of love and forgiveness. Meanwhile the "Christian nations" of Europe were preparing their most terrible orgy of hate.

During the whole of July 1914, no post or newspapers were received in Lambaréné. Only through a scribbled note brought by Joseph from a neighbouring factory, whose manager had been asked to take a package of medicines on the next steamer to Cape Lopez, did Schweitzer learn that in Europe mobilization had been ordered and that a state of war probably already existed. The river-steamer had to be placed at the disposal of the government authorities and no one knew when it would go to Cape Lopez.

On August 5 something happened which made the facts clear in the most brutal way: a deputy from the chief authority of the French province appeared with the command: "Dr. Albert Schweitzer and his wife are subjects of the German emperor. They must be regarded as prisoners and may not leave their house until further notice. All intercourse with the outside world is forbidden."

Schweitzer submitted in silence to his fate. The fact that he,

Carrying his own luggage during a visit to France, 1952

With his cat, Lambaréné, 1947

who only came out to this French colony because he wanted to help sick men, should now be caged in like a dangerous animal seemed to him no less senseless than the war itself.

The doctor's patients did not take the sudden suspension of his activities quite so calmly. They gathered together before his house and abused the soldiers who kept watch there. Gradually the severity of this house imprisonment was eased. Schweitzer took up his normal medical work again. In the weeks of enforced and unaccustomed idleness, no longer being able to treat sick men, he had been taking the pulse of the sick age, turning his stethoscope on to the heart of western civilization, patiently drawing a fever chart of an ominous and fatal decline in the creative powers of Europe.

And he wrote down the following reflections:

At the present moment war is raging as the result of the decline of Western culture. . . . In the world of modern thought, a tragic event is taking place,—the slow but irresistible process by which the original nexus between world- and life-affirmation and on the other hand the realm of ethics is being loosened and will finally be broken. It comes to this, that European humanity is being moulded by the determination to progress in a purely external sense and has lost all sense of ultimate ends. . . . The question is this: how could it happen that the modern world-view with its life-affirming emphasis and its non-moral ends should have developed from an original moral and spiritual outlook? The process is explainable only on the hypothesis that it is not really rooted in thought. (From *My Life and Thought*.)

The first war-time newspapers and illustrated papers that reached Schweitzer only deepened his sorrow. He wrote on the large sheets of paper on which he was drawing up his Philosophy of Civilization:

There is still no evidence of any insight into the causes of our spiritual agony. Year by year the spread of opinions by collective groups goes on while freedom of individual thought is crushed in the process. . . . With the free expression of individual thought modern man also surrenders the power of independent moral judgement. He suppresses the doubts which arise in his mind in order to be able to approve of what the group prescribes in word and deed. . . . Thus his own judgment is lost in that of the masses and his moral sense is abased to the level of theirs. As a result of this process he is capable of condoning all that is senseless, harsh, unjust, and evil in the procedure of his country. . . . If among modern men we find so few who preserve intact their human and moral feelings not the least important reason is that they constantly sacrifice their independent moral personality on the altar of the fatherland. . . . (From *Civilization and Ethics*.)

When he was freed from house arrest Schweitzer at first hardly dared to speak to his African friends living in the district. They must now be deriding him, the white man, who could speak so eloquently about the necessity of forgiving seventy times seven.

But just in this situation Schweitzer experienced the inborn goodness of heart of these primitive men. There was not one who called him a liar, not one who accosted him sternly with such remarks as: "Why do you appeal to us to live in accordance with the gospel of love when your own countrymen do not do so?"

But Schweitzer was careful to see that the illustrated magazines sent from home showing pictures of the self-laceration of Europe did not fall into the hands of the Africans.

The first Christmas of the war drew near. In the doctor's house it had grown quite dark when Schweitzer lit the candles of the Christmas tree, one after another. It was not a fir-tree, but a palm-tree, beneath which an unpretentious gift table was laid. Silent and thoughtful, Schweitzer and his wife gazed at the lights. When the candles were half burnt down the doctor blew them out with a big puff. "They are our only candles. And they must do for next year too."

Many a good friend had already fallen, and for months the war had been raging in their native Alsace, carrying fire and destruction in its train. Heavy guns were roaring on the mountain-slopes all round Günsbach. The fir-forests of the Lingenkopf now consisted of bare white stumps or charred ones. Mountain pastures which had formerly been excursion places for the Schweitzer family were now mass graves.

Schweitzer did not believe in a speedy end to the war. He saw that new weapons would not bring about any swifter decision, but only exact more sacrifices. He had no faith in the belief that the war was being fought to finish all wars. The evil was too deep-seated.

Unfortunately Albert Schweitzer was right in his pessimistic prognosis about the length of the war. Even on the Ogowe, thousands of miles away from the scene of this convulsive world conflict, the consequences of war began to make themselves felt. The Africans complained about the increasing scarcity of provisions. The colonial authority pressed black men into the armed forces: they had to serve as carriers in the struggle which was going on in the nearby Cameroons. When the river-steamer departed, weeping wives and mothers came down to the landing stage.

By chance Albert Schweitzer witnessed one such scene. An old negro woman sat on a stone by the river-side. The trail of smoke from the steamer on which her son had left had long ago vanished behind the tall trees of the jungle, but still she remained on the spot where he had last embraced her, silently weeping. The white man sat beside her and took her hand. In stammering words he tried to comfort her. But she sobbed more and more, as if she had not heard him.

"Suddenly, I felt that I was weeping with her, weeping in silence with the rays of the setting sun streaming all around us."

The carrying away of so many men who were used to hunting had some unforeseen consequences. Now there were not enough elephant-hunters to prevent the elephants from getting into the sown fields and gardens. Herds of twenty or more beasts stormed by night into the banana plantations to the north-west of Lambaréné: they ravaged and destroyed everything, ate up the fruit, and trampled down the stalks. The result was a dearth of food in the whole district. Helene Schweitzer had to be endlessly careful with the little store of food that remained. People became more and more accustomed to eating the rather sweet flesh of monkeys.

To crown these misfortunes, Schweitzer discovered one day that the white ants had got into the reserve chests of food. Everything had to be unpacked and packed up again. Helene Schweitzer learned how to solder. For hours on end she sealed boxes of flour and maize with the bluish flame of the solder lamp. In many cases it was already too late. The eggs of tiny weevils had already got into the boxes, turning them into dust.

It sometimes seemed to Schweitzer that some of his friends in Europe had lost their reason. Otherwise how could they write so enthusiastically both from Germany and France about their "holy war"? In these circumstances he found it refreshing to hear the lonely voice of his old friend Romain Rolland, who tried to raise himself above the din of battle in an article in the Swiss *Journal de Genève* entitled "Au dessus de la Mêlée", in which he condemned the short-sighted fanaticism on both sides of the Rhine. There formed around Romain Rolland a small group of strong independent minds linked with each other by correspondence. This group consisted of the Austrian poet Stefan Zweig, the French sculptor Auguste Rodin, the English philosopher Bertrand Russell, the Irish playwright George Bernard Shaw, the German scientist Albert Einstein and the Alsatian Albert Schweitzer.

The lonely man in Lambaréné felt an imperative need to write from the jungle and express his sympathy with Romain Rolland, execrated by the mass of French public opinion as a Judas. In the late summer of 1915 he wrote to his distant friend, to whom he was bound by an affinity of outlook:

Dear Friend,
   You know perhaps that I am interned here. After being strictly guarded for three and a half months by native soldiers, my situation was eased and some freedom of movement and the permission to continue my medical practice was given me. My health is fairly good and I have enough to eat. Only I am feeling very conscious of having spent two and a half years on the equator and my wife feels the same about it. However I am really writing to you simply in order to tell you that I read now and then what you have written. The newspapers reach me in the

isolation of the jungle, and your thoughts are to me one of the few comforting things in these sad times. In view of all that you know of me you must realise how sympathetic we are in ideas and outlook. And I must tell you how much I admire your courage in swimming against the stream of the vulgarity into which the fanatical thinking of the masses is now falling. Do not bother to reply to this forlorn greeting from the primeval forest, you have certainly much more important writing to do. If however you should ever write to me remember that other people might read your letter, before it reaches me. Good-bye—for how long? Fight well in a cause in which I am whole-heartedly with you, though incapable in my present position of giving you active assistance.

With cordial greetings,
Yours,
Albert Schweitzer.

A second letter, written in the October of the same year, strengthened still further the bond of spiritual sympathy which united the two friends of peace:

Dear Friend,
I have received your letter of Sunday. I see that you have lost many friends on whom you thought that you were able to count. Hence those who understand you must love you still more because you remained human, they must give you yet more marked expression of their affection and sympathy. An enormous task lies before us if we are to create a new mentality. You will always find me at your side in this. . . . Thank you for the news about the musicians. Every word from you is like beautiful organ music in my loneliness.

Yours ever,
Albert Schweitzer.

To feel himself not quite isolated in his views which were completely opposed to the fanatical patriotism of the peoples gave Albert Schweitzer renewed courage to go on with his critical essay on culture after his hard day's work. Certainly the world was still covered in darkness, but he could already see arising scattered gleams of the light of reason and humanity. Were they evanescent flickers or the steady glow of beacon lights? Would they be blown out by the ill wind? Whatever might be the truth of it, Schweitzer avoided such sceptical questions. He felt it each day to be a great privilege that while others must kill, he could save life, and that furthermore he could work with his pen for the coming age of peace.

CHAPTER 13

War Years in the Primeval Forest

THE INSIGHT WHICH came to Albert Schweitzer in his search for a healing vision such as would recreate Western culture must be characterized by no less a term than revelation. He has himself described this mystical experience with supreme clarity and penetration in *My Life and Thought*:

> For months I went on living in a state of unceasing inner turmoil. Without reaching any conclusions and without suffering any interruption to my work in the hospital my thought persistently revolved around the question of the inner relation between world- and life-affirmation and the moral consciousness. I wandered round and round in a thicket where I could find no path. I pushed against an iron door which would not yield. . . .

Just then he had to take a river voyage to attend a missionary's sick wife. It was September 1915.

> We crawled slowly upstream, laboriously groping our way between sandbanks, for it was the dry season. I sat musing on the deck of the tow boat, striving to come to grips with the elemental and universal idea of the ethical which I had never found genuinely expressed in any philosophical system.
>
> I wrote page after page of disconnected thoughts simply in order that my attention should remain concentrated on the problem before me. On the evening of the third day just as we were passing through a herd of hippopotamuses and the sun was setting, there suddenly and imperiously confronted me, unsought and unexpected by myself, the key-phrase Reverence for Life. The iron gates had yielded; the pathway in the thicket was now visible.
>
> Now I had penetrated to the idea which embraced both world- and life-affirmation and the moral consciousness. Now I knew

that the world view of ethical life-affirmation together with the cultural ideals which spring from it, is rooted in philosophical reflection.

He began now to plan his great work on the philosophy of civilization. It was to be divided into four parts:

> *First :* Concerning the lack of culture at the present time and its fundamental causes. *Second :* A consideration of the idea of Reverence for Life in relation to previous essays in European philosophy. *Third :* An exposition of the world view involved in the idea of Reverence for Life. *Fourth :* Concerning the culture-state.

Schweitzer usually worked near the open door of his room which led out on to the latticed veranda. There he could feel the cool of the gentle evening breeze. Some days he went straight out on to the veranda to work, where he could not only write, but afterwards arrange his camp bed for the night if—as so often happened—he had given up his room to a white man whom he was treating. Planters, wood merchants, employees of the neighbouring factories came to the doctor more frequently than before to get toned up after more than two years—on account of the war—of the moist heat of Equatorial Africa.

Lambaréné in fact was quite overrun by European patients. Instead of going to the much nearer military hospital at Cape Lopez they came up the river to consult Schweitzer. "Fortunately I still have a stock of condensed milk for the sick," Schweitzer wrote home.

The doctor later made an interesting observation in *On the Edge of the Primeval Forest* as a result of his contact with other white men.

> The educated man—strange as this may sound—bears the life of the jungle better than the uneducated because he has resources of refreshment which are unknown to the latter. In reading a good book he ceases to be the thing which wears itself out the whole day long in struggling against the unreliability of the natives and the importunity of beasts. He becomes a man once

more. I pity the poor fellow who cannot again come to himself in this environment, and thus regain strength. He perishes because he is crushed by the terrible prose of Africa.

Schweitzer's own sovereign remedy for weariness of life lay in the huge parcels of books which Professor Strohl of Zürich sent out to him every month through the Red Cross. He delighted again in the philosophical works of the eighteenth century. It seemed to him that since that age philosophy had increasingly shrunk from its great task of formulating cultural ideals.

While he writes in his room or on the veranda, the orange-speckled toads and crickets strike up their nightly symphony, often drowned by the screeching and roaring coming from the forest. Under the table lies the tame pygmy antelope, the "Antilöpeli", which now and then bumps its pretty horns against the heavy boots of its master. Not far away its inseparable friend, the dog Caramaba, prowls around snarling; if he yelps too loudly or tries to entice his master away from his work into playing, by whining and jumping up, then Schweitzer calls out, "Do be good and quiet, I am just writing something precisely about you."

Nor was this a lie. Albert Schweitzer, the friend of animals, was in fact in the process of admitting into the luxurious chambers of philosophy hitherto reserved for man all four-legged and winged creatures. His reverence for life was not confined to respect for all human life, but included every living creature. He writes in *My Life and Thought*:

> The great defect of all previous ethical systems was that they thought their concern was only with the behaviour of man to man. . . . Man proves his moral stature only when the kingdom of life as such, embracing plants and animals as well as men, is sacred to him and he devotes himself in service to all life that is in need. . .

"But do I not myself kill noxious vermin? Do I not shoot

plundering birds? Do I not at times eat meat?" Schweitzer
asks himself.

"Yes, that is true. One being maintains itself at the expense of
another, one destroys the other. Only in the thinking man has
the will-to-live become enlightened and reflective and truly
humane. But man cannot completely carry out this ideal because
man too is subject to the cruel law of self-preservation at the expense of others, implying ever-accumulating guilt. In so far as
he is truly ethical man strives as much as possible to escape this
necessity. . . . He longs to be able to prove his humanity and feels
obliged to bring release from suffering.

One day an African woman came to the doctor with a tame
boar—two months old.

"Take it," she urged the doctor; "it will run after you like a
dog."

After a moment's hesitation Schweitzer decided to accept the
offer, for it was quite clear to him that otherwise the animal
would be roasted on the spit the same evening. Hardly had the
doctor purchased his new guest for the sum of five francs, when
he regretted his decision. For he had promised his wife most
solemnly that without her approval he would not make any
further additions to his private zoo. In spite of his wife's dis-
approval, Josephine the red-haired boar became Schweitzer's
most faithful companion. While the doctor was working in
the hospital she loved to wander around in the mission church.
"As soon as ever the bell rang she would rush off to church,"
Schweitzer later was pleased to relate to his Alsatian friends. "I
think she has never missed any of the schoolchildren's morning
or evening prayers."

But at the Sunday service Josephine behaved badly. In
Lambaréné people were quite accustomed to the fact that not
only men but animals also wandered during service time into
the corrugated-iron building which served as a church. Since
the doors remained open, dogs, hens, wethers, and goats came
and went, unconcerned about the sacred offices.

One Sunday Josephine came straight from the mire where she

had been snugly grunting and rooting around, and, dripping with black slime, rushed right into the middle of the congregation. Schweitzer still remembered the incident with a humorous shudder: "And now she went pushing her way through the benches of the children who drew their knees up to their necks —now she came to the women—now to the men—now to the other missionary—now to the ladies of the mission with their white frocks against which she tried to rub herself clean—now to the doctor's wife—now to myself. At that moment she received her first kick from me and it was a good one . . ."

She would creep into the children's dormitories and intrude herself on them as a most unwelcome sleeping companion. She would stretch herself under the best mosquito net and sleep on cleanly made-up beds, but worst of all, as soon as Josephine was half a year old complaints came from all quarters that hens were disappearing; which meant the end of Josephine.

When Schweitzer came to Lambaréné it had been his intention not to burden himself with domestic animals, as so many other Europeans did. He successfully withstood the temptation to receive into his house a chimpanzee offered him by a young European as a gift. But then came the story of the parrot, and resistance was no longer possible. This bird was given to Schweitzer by a native cook as a kind of peace offering. To refuse it would have hurt the man's feelings. Hence it remained in the house and soon there was a second and a third parrot.

There was, for example, Kudeku, who came into the possession of the Schweitzers with a magnificent vocabulary of racy French words of abuse. It was painfully difficult to wean him from his habit of greeting everyone with his resonant cry of "*cochon*" ("pig") or "*saligaud*" ("dirty swine"). Still worse were the tricks of Sakku, the other parrot. He watched and listened for the doctor's wife when in the mornings she would feed the hens with caressing phrases like: "Come along, Bibi, bibi, bibii . . ." and could soon imitate her so perfectly that the fowls would come running up in great excitement every time Sakku began calling: "Come along, Bibi . . ." It was his special delight every time his cage was opened to hop over immediately to the dog Caramaba, still sleeping after his faithful night watch, and to wake him by a bite in his thigh. "As I was very sorry for the dog," Schweitzer once reported to an amused audience, "I would get up as soon as my wife opened the parrot cage and run behind the house to wake him."

Schweitzer greatly delighted in his antelopes. He loved the two dwarf antelopes Samba and Antilöpeli so much that he even took them with him on a short holiday which he spent with his wife at Cape Lopez. When in the summer of 1915 Schweitzer received as a gift his first little antelope, an uncommonly tender and graceful creature, he was warned that such animals were not to be brought up indoors because condensed milk gave them diarrhœa, from which they died. But, as so often before, the optimism of Schweitzer was justified. He always mixed a little drop of opium with the milk in the feeding-bottle and the difficulties which had been prophesied did not come to pass.

The fact that this animal, which the negroes regarded as the shyest of all jungle creatures, followed the doctor about like a little dog and ate out of his wife's hand did much in the eyes of the natives to enhance still further the prestige of the Schweitzers. Often they came to Lambaréné merely to see this miracle for themselves.

Still more astonishing was the fact that a second small antelope became a companion to the first. It was the gift of a planter whose dog had brought her home half dead. Samba—as the antelope was called—became acclimatized to the doctor's house only with the greatest difficulty, for, unlike Antilöpeli, she had once known the full freedom of the forest. But soon she too was eating out of the hand of the doctor's wife and tenderly nibbling round the soles of the doctor's shoes when at night he sat writing his manuscript.

Another antelope, of normal size, which Schweitzer reared in his home was called Clas.

This antelope brought me the reputation of being a very good son, relates the doctor in a magazine story. It happened in this wise: When one morning it accompanied me into the hospital, an old negro woman took me aside. "Doctor," she said, "your antelope is already big and fat. You must eat it now." "Not just yet," I replied. The next day she asked me again why I did not yet kill and eat the animal. The negroes do not understand why one should have an edible beast and not eat it. Again I replied evasively. After a few more days she returned to the subject. In order to quieten her once for all I told her that I was proposing to take the animal with me to Europe. Then she gathered other women round her and said to them: "Listen all of you, see what a good son the doctor is. He wants to take the antelope with him to Europe in order to eat it with his mother."

Roast antelope would not have been unwelcome in Günsbach in 1916, for even in the happy valley food was beginning to get scarce. Lodging and food had to be found for the troops in every district, and the Günsbach parsonage was partly requisitioned.

It was fortunate for the doctor's parents that a manufacturer named Kiener, who lived close by in the village of Walbach, sometimes invited the clergyman and his wife to sit down at his table, which even in wartime was plentifully furnished. On July 3, 1916, the pastor and his seventy-four-year-old wife walked over to Walbach, a distance of two and a half miles there and back, for no public vehicle was available during the war.

It was probably about four o'clock in the afternoon. The two old people, with no thought of trouble, were nearly home when they were met by a German soldier on horseback. Quite inexplicably the horse suddenly shied, tore away at a gallop, and before Pastor Schweitzer could pull his wife aside, the animal had knocked her down. She struck her head with such violence on the pavement that she became unconscious. Farmers who were passing by fetched a rack-wagon out of the nearest house and took the seriously injured woman to her home in Günsbach. There she died at eleven o'clock that night as the result of a severely fractured skull without regaining consciousness.

For many days Albert Schweitzer was numb with grief at the news. War had taken his mother from him in such a brutal way, and it must have tortured him especially to think that it was an animal that had caused her death.

The Schweitzers had now been in Lambaréné for more than three years, one year longer than the period for which Europeans found it possible to endure the climate of Equatorial Africa. Already the doctor and his wife were complaining of tropical anæmia—a type of anæmia which manifests itself in severe symptoms of lassitude. The short distance which he had to climb from the hospital to the house exhausted him as much as a mountain-climbing expedition would, although it only took four minutes. His nerves were getting taut. The smallest vexation caused him to raise his voice in a flare of anger, and reduced his wife to tears.

The doctor also had to resign himself to a deep personal disappointment. His Joseph, who was accustomed to describe himself proudly as Dr. Albert Schweitzer's chief medical assistant, left him because of a temporarily unavoidable decrease in his salary.

News of the war arrived in Lambaréné only once a fortnight. Then there came to the door of the house or the hospital a native soldier with an assortment of telegrams which had come in at Cape Lopez or Libreville. This single sheet had to be glanced through quickly, for the messenger carried the same bulletin to two or three dozen other factories, farms, and mission stations.

Every time the post came, the cook Aloys put his fat face round the door of the living-room.

"Doctor, is the war still on?" he would ask.

"Yes, Aloys, there is still a war on."

One morning in September 1917, as so many times before, the native postman stood before the door, but this time he brought not a bulletin of war news, but an official order, which ran:

"Dr. Albert Schweitzer and his wife are to be taken to Europe to a prisoner of war camp by the next available ship."

Schweitzer had for a long time expected this, but had secretly hoped that he would be spared. However, the longer the war lasted the more severe became the measures taken by both sides to deal with nationals of opposing countries. The ever-mounting tide of hate would brook no exceptions. Schweitzer surrendered himself to an apparently unavoidable fate, borne up by the positive hope of being able gradually to transform it by spiritual resources from within.

The whole mission helped in the packing up. Sakku, the impudent parrot, looked on and croaked out his disrespectful comments. But when he saw that the rooms were becoming more and more empty, and that the doctor's wife could find no time even to feed her hens, and the doctor no longer whistled for Caramaba at the midday meal to throw him scraps of bones and fish, the intelligent little creature began to realize that something extraordinary was happening. First of all Sakku grew silent with grief and refused to eat. Then his feathers began to bristle up, twitchings set in, and the faithful bird ended his life in convulsions. Many tears were shed over him, and every day his friendly enemy Caramaba crept around the little grave in the missionary garden. Kudeku, the other parrot, was far less sentimental. He didn't at all mind biting to pieces the doctor's gold pen, which he had unwisely left lying on the table.

For two whole nights Schweitzer worked to make a short extract from his extensive sketches and essays about the decline and restoration of civilization. For he would not trust taking the original manuscript with him into internment. The chances were that it might be confiscated by some furious official and perhaps destroyed. He drew up the following maxims which crystallized the essence of his new doctrine concerning reverence for life:

> The man who has developed spiritual and reflective powers considers as good:
> To preserve life.
> To promote life.
> To bring all evolving life to its highest degree of development.
>
> The man who has developed spiritual and reflective powers considers as evil:
> To destroy life.
> To injure life.
> To fetter evolving life.

The original and already very substantial text of his work Schweitzer committed to the safe keeping of an American missionary named Ford, who had been transferred to Lambaréné from Libreville.

What a heaven-sent blessing that the *Afrique* on which the Schweitzers were to be deported was delayed a few days! There was time for all the medicines and surgical instruments to be soldered and sealed in cases and put safely in storage.

Two days before his departure a patient was brought to him suffering from strangulated hernia. If the doctor did not intervene at once the poor man would certainly die in torment. The cases were quickly reopened to get out the most essential instruments, and with hands trembling from fatigue and overwrought nerves, and for the last time, so far as he could see, Albert Schweitzer saved the life of one of his African brothers.

The people stood weeping on the river-bank as the Schweitzers went on board the river-steamer. At this last moment the Father Superior of the Roman Catholic mission appeared to say farewell. Warmly he pressed the hand of his "German enemy" and sturdy Protestant colleague.

The *Alembe* pushes off. Once again the waves, tears, cries of longing and hope. Is it "Farewell, Lambaréné," or "*Au revoir*, Lambaréné?"

With his antelopes

The "high street", Lambaréné. Instruments are sterilized in the outdoor stove with brick chimneys on the right. (*Right*) In the hospital pharmacy. Supplies from Europe or America have to be ordered six months to a year ahead

CHAPTER 14

A Very Different Europe

SCHWEITZER TRAVELLED TO Europe in the already decrepit steamer *Afrique*, which only two years later sank in a storm in the Bay of Biscay. His destination was an internment camp. He was now a number, a paper in a file of documents, an object of bureaucratic discipline, in short a man of the twentieth century.

Little more than four years had passed since he made his hopeful journey along the same route. This time all meals had to be taken in his cabin, and he was seen on deck by the other passengers only at certain hours and under military guard. For hours on end he practised Bach fugues and Widor's sixth organ symphony, using just an ordinary table, but provided in his imagination with all the necessary manuals, registers, and even with an organ pedal-board. And on these imaginary manuals he practised finger exercises in unending variation.

After landing at Bordeaux the Schweitzers were first quartered in a dingy barracks which served as a halting place on the way to their internment camp. They found it cold and draughty, and for the first time for many years Albert Schweitzer was ill, with diarrhœa as a result of the bad prison food.

The Governor of the camp in the Pyrenees district to which they were transferred was full of kindness and sympathy towards them. He had formerly been in the colonies, and tried as far as he could to make life tolerable for the civilian internees under his authority.

It was no easy task in the camp at Garaison, where hundreds of nationals of the Central Powers, who happened to be living in France or the French colonies at the outbreak of the war, were shut up in an old convent which had not been inhabited for years. In winter the long stone passages and most of the bedrooms were always stark cold because there was no sort of heating apparatus. Almost continuous rain, and monotonous food, depressed the internees. Many of them were married to Frenchwomen, and their children could speak only French. France, where they had built up the structure of their lives, had become an enemy country for them, while their native lands of Germany or Austria were foreign. Schweitzer describes in eloquent terms this small involuntary association of peoples in *My Life and Thought*:

> To anyone who was in fairly good health of mind and body this prison camp offered a spectacle of varied interest in that you could meet there men of many nationalities and almost every trade and occupation. It sheltered: scholars and artists, especially painters who had been caught by the war while still in Paris; German and Austrian shoemakers and ladies' tailors, who had worked in the big Parisian firms; bank managers, hotel managers, waiters, engineers, architects, artisans, and tradesmen who were established in France or its colonies; Catholic missionaries and members of religious orders from the Sahara who wore the red fez with their white garments; merchants from Liberia and other regions of the West African coast; business people from North America, South America, China, and India who had been captured on the high seas; crews of German and Austrian cargo boats which had suffered the same fate; Turks, Arabians, Greeks, and members of the Balkan countries who for some reason or other had been deported to the Middle East during the course of the war, among them Turks with veiled women. What a multi-coloured picture was presented by the assembly in the courtyard which took place twice daily!
> In order to broaden one's mind there was no need to read books in the camp. For the book of life stood open to the perusal of intelligent men. I made rich use of this unique opportunity of learning. I acquired a knowledge of the working of banks, architecture, the construction of mills, and the life of millers, of corn growing and the construction of stoves and many other things which otherwise I would never have known anything about.

While most of the internees suffered from their enforced idleness in the camp, there were two groups who did not feel the slightest discomfort—the sailors and the Hungarian gypsy musicians. Schweitzer was enthusiastically admitted into the musicians' fellowship, practised with them in the loft, showed them how he played every day on his imaginary organ (which was still merely a simple table). He never forgot the serenade which the former elegant café orchestra played to his wife on the morning of her birthday, and how the romantic waltz from the *Tales of Hoffmann* echoed through the bare stone passages of the former convent.

The Schweitzers were eventually moved to a camp for Alsatians in the convent of St. Paul de Mausole, near St. Rémy in Provence, and not far from Arles. Here Schweitzer found an old harmonium which he played with astonishing success on Sundays for both the Christian confessions. The Protestants attended the Catholic rite and the Catholics took part in the Evangelical service in order to hear the organ twice over.

In St. Rémy Schweitzer had an unusual experience. In the bare convent he encountered the shade of another great man. Immediately after his arrival, the iron stove, with its pipes running the length of the main room, seemed to Schweitzer remarkably familiar. He wondered where he could have seen it before. And then the connection suddenly occurred to him. The convent had been a mental hospital and Vincent Van Gogh had once been a patient. Van Gogh had used the magic of his pencil and paint-brush to convey the iron stove to posterity. Like the Schweitzers, he had frozen on the cold stone floor when the mistral blew.

At St. Rémy Schweitzer often doubted the rationality of his fellow men. The fierce hatred stirred up by the war had affected the inhabitants of this southern French village as a sort of collective mania. When the internees appeared on the streets they were pursued with words of abuse, fists were clenched and stones flew. Schweitzer, however, behaved as if he noticed nothing of all that. He often went down into the old town with its narrow streets in order to talk with an old man who had known Van Gogh during the year when he had been confined in the mental home, and he gave medical help when needed.

On July 12, 1918, the Schweitzers left St. Rémy for Alsace on an exchange of internees arranged through Switzerland. Heavily laden with luggage and parcels they struggled over the gravelled railway at Tarascon to an engine-shed a long way outside the station, where they were to wait until the train was ready. Each step on the sharp-edged stones was a torment. Then someone offered to help them carry their things. It was a cripple whom the doctor had once treated in the camp. The poor fellow had almost no luggage himself, because practically nothing was left to him.

"Deeply moved, I accepted his help," Schweitzer wrote later in his autobiography. "While we went forward side by side in the burning heat of the sun I vowed, in memory of him, to look out on all railway stations in future to see whether I could help heavily loaded travellers."

Once again, as when they travelled so eagerly from Paris to Bordeaux at the beginning of their African voyage, the Schweitzers were impressed by the beauty of the French landscape. But the land was not so bright now as it had been in the year 1913; everything bore the signs of wear and tear, the carriages were hacked and torn, rusty, dirty, and smeared with the gloomy colours of camouflage. Tanks and guns were being moved to repair workshops behind the front. And on the platforms of the railway stations through which they passed were wounded men, women in mourning, and nurses.

Somewhere between Tarascon and Lyons the Schweitzers experienced a comic episode arising from confusion of names, which suddenly invested with a touch of irony the tragic happenings of the time. A group of friendly ladies and gentlemen rushed up to the internees at a small station and led them to tables richly spread for a feast. There was roast chicken, good burgundy, cold pie, and chocolate. The meal was intended for French internees from northern France, who were going to the south of France for a holiday after their release from Germany. When the station-master announced that the "*train des internés*" had just arrived, the hosts naturally supposed that it had on board the people they were looking for. As the Germans ate the food provided for the French, everyone laughed at the misunderstanding, but Schweitzer felt they were also laughing at the crazy spirit of their age.

Passing through beautiful, untouched Switzerland, the Schweitzers arrived at Constance, where Professor Bresslau and his wife came to meet them. Helene Schweitzer was allowed to travel on with her parents to Strasbourg immediately. But the doctor, like all male members of his party, had to remain behind in Constance to undergo the formalities. He did not arrive in Strasbourg till late the following night. The town was shrouded in the thickest darkness. In the black moonless night Schweitzer groped his way through the familiar streets.

The cathedral? St. Nicholas? St. William's church? They were all strangely disguised by sandbags. The glass windows had been taken out and replaced by wooden boards. It was too late to think of going to the house of the Bresslau family, who now lived in a suburb, so he found his way to Frau Fisher's house hard by St. Thomas's, where the door opened to his knocking. The kind brave woman, who had once been indispensable to him when he was making his preparations for his African journey, stood now like a dark shadow on the threshold, and welcomed him back.

To get home to Günsbach Schweitzer had to walk the nine miles from Colmar, for the local railway was not working on account of the war and the nearness of the front. He describes his return in his autobiography:

This, then, was the peaceful valley of which I had taken leave on that Good Friday of 1913. There was a dull thud of heavy gunfire from the hills. In the streets you walked between wire gratings stuffed with straw as between high walls. This was intended to conceal the life and commerce of the valley from the enemy batteries planted on the ridge of the Vosges. Everywhere were walled up trenches for machine guns. Houses shot to bits. Mountains which I remembered as covered with trees stood bare. Only a few isolated trunks here and there had been spared by the shelling. In the villages an official order was posted that gas masks must be carried.

Günsbach, the last inhabited place before the trenches, owed it to the mountains between which it nestled that it had not long been destroyed by the artillery on the Vosges. In the midst of many soldiers and with ruined houses all around them the inhabitants went about their business as if there were no war. It was as much a matter of course to them that they should bring their second hay crop home only at night as that when the alarm sounded they should dive into the cellar or that at any moment they might be commanded to leave at once both the village and their belongings on account of a threatened enemy attack. My father had grown so indifferent to all danger that instead of going into the cellar with the others when the shelling was on, he remained in his room. He could hardly now picture to himself a time when he had not shared his parsonage with officers and soldiers.

Schweitzer's health, which had been much impaired since the diarrhœa infection at Bordeaux, completely collapsed at Günsbach. He lay in a high fever in that bedroom at the parsonage where once he had been so happy. There was no transport to Strasbourg for treatment, so Schweitzer dragged himself again along the country road to Colmar. After over three miles, deathly pale, he got a lift in a cart. On September 1, 1918, the surgeon Schweitzer was operated on in the Strasbourg university clinic. And his Strasbourg friends wondered what was to become of the man whose life work in Africa had been ruined by the war.

CHAPTER 15

Editor and Lecturer

ONCE AGAIN FRIENDS came forward to help. Schwander, Strasbourg's warm-hearted mayor, offered Schweitzer a post as assistant at the Department of Skin Diseases in the town hospital, and the faithful congregation of St. Nicholas invited him back as curate, and gave him the use of the parsonage house at 5, St. Nicholas Quayside.

In spite of all this, however, Schweitzer could not feel really cheerful and confident about the future. There weighed on his conscience the burden of debt in which he had inevitably become involved during the war years in order to keep his forest hospital going. How could he ever pay it back? By appeals? But that was not to be thought of as long as the war lasted. And after the war? But then both in Germany and France there would be more immediate and pressing problems to claim the attention of generous people than the old debts of an African missionary hospital. Schweitzer had also lost contact with his friends in Paris, Switzerland, England, and Spain. Later he summed up his mood at that time by saying that he felt like an old penny that had rolled under a piece of furniture and got lost there.

When finally, in November 1918, the bells rang out at the end of the war, Schweitzer could not fall in with the mood of general rejoicing and hope which greeted the new peace. He felt that the statesmen of the victorious nations were complying too readily with the unreasonable wishes of the peoples who had very understandably grown bitter and hard as a result of the long-drawn-out war. Thus the seeds of new conflict were sown.

Alsace, for instance, which only yesterday was violently germanified, was now to be equally violently frenchified by its new masters. Both pastors of St. Nicholas were suspended from preaching until further notice. One of them, named Pastor Gerold, who had been dismissed by the Germans for some supposedly anti-German remarks dropped during the war, was examined by the French to ensure his reliability, while the other, Pastor Ernst, was compelled to resign his post because of his insufficiently pro-French outlook.

The Schweitzer family, too, were hard hit by the old fanaticism in its latest form, when Helene's father, Harry Bresslau, was ordered to quit Strasbourg without delay. The ageing scholar's sole crime was to have edited and supervised a section of the *Monumenta Germaniae Historica*, whose object was research into the sources of German history—and to have done this in Strasbourg. For the new Governor appointed from Paris, this was enough to justify immediate expulsion. On December 1, 1918, Professor Bresslau, sometime Rector of the University of Strasbourg, together with his wife, crossed the Kehl bridge into Germany on foot, ruthlessly driven from their beautiful home.

How much more dismayed would Schweitzer have been could he have known at that time what was to be the future fate of his father-in-law? In the next war, at the order of the Nazis, the mortal remains of the Jew Harry Bresslau, who died in 1926, were disinterred from the cemetery at Heidelberg and summarily transferred to a field for the mass burial of non-Aryans. To have been banished by the chauvinists of the left bank of the Rhine for his Germanizing tendencies, and to have been deemed unworthy to rest in a German graveyard by the racial fanatics on the right bank was a cruel destiny for Harry Bresslau.

But when Schweitzer's first child, his daughter Rhena, was born on his own forty-fourth birthday, January 14, 1919, he took it as the kindling of a special beacon of hope. He wrote in the *Church Messenger for Alsace-Lorraine* for January 3, 1920:

You do not know what to think of the old year. It was a difficult time for all, for you perhaps your most difficult time, for it denied you what you thought you were entitled to expect from it, and brought you new distress and anxiety for which you were not prepared. It may have taken from you your wealth, perhaps even your home, have caused you to lose friends and to gain enemies, have shaken your faith in humanity, have disrupted the normal foundations of your life, have torn from you by death those who were most dear to you, and have delivered you up to the scorn and malicious gossip of men.

Nevertheless do not take leave of the old year with grumbling and complaining, but wrestle with it as—according to that mysterious narrative of scripture—our forefather Jacob wrestled with the angel and wrung from it a blessing. Wrestle with the year, do not wrangle with it. Every year is bestowed upon us that it may not merely bring us forward in the time of our earthly life but enable us to progress also in our inner life. It leads us on to eternity and is meant to prepare us for eternity. But this process of preparation and ripening means that we experience the sunshine, the rain, and the storms of life and through it all grow in the inner man. Know this and ponder on it. Step out of the turmoil of the world and climb to the mountain tops of the spirit, invoke your purest thoughts, invoke Jesus and call upon God and then set out your summing up of the old year.

Do not forget where you ought to begin—with an expression of thanksgiving. Through all your distresses God has brought forth for you something good where you least expected it. Think back attentively over the year that is past and see how much cause for gratitude you have and it will become illuminated by lights which when you were traversing that time you did not perceive, just as by long gazing at the heavens one little star after another appears whereas previously you had seen only darkness.

This New Year message was one of the many leading articles and commentaries which Schweitzer wrote for the *Church Messenger* in the first two years after the war and which at that time appeared weekly under his editorship. Up to now his many biographers have neglected the fact that among his numerous other occupations he was also at times a journalist.

Not only did he know as an editor how to make his journal

amusing and readable by poems, anecdotes, short stories, and Chinese-like proverbs, but he also distinguished himself by the energy and firmness of the positions he adopted towards questions of the day. He defended, for example, a Berlin teacher who had aroused the opposition of the school authorities by the mildness and kindness of his methods. Or he took up his pen in order to write an article about the unfortunate position of French Protestantism, in the course of which he made some prophetic remarks calculated to promote a downright revolution in the conception of a professional clergy:

> Today the clergyman expects that the church will provide him with the means of livelihood. It will do so to an ever diminishing extent. We are moving towards a complete revolution of society. The old ideas about everything, from the family to private property, are changing. Productive work is now the law for all. In this new ordering of society there will be no room for professions whose representatives appear as idlers. If the churches can no longer support their clergy it is a sign that the clergy are no longer capable of maintaining the church as a prosperous institution.
>
> The parson as an officer of the church has outlived his usefulness. He must engage in new evangelical experiments. Our people must be won over afresh for the gospel. The minister must be capable of performing this service for his people and thus setting an example of productive work. Moreover this would be nothing new but simply a return to the original sources and spirit of primitive Christianity. Jesus and the apostles were artisans and lived by their toil. And our missionaries must be similarly qualified craftsmen.
>
> Under such circumstances will men still be found who possess enough faith and idealism to sacrifice their future with such ill-assured prospects to the service of the church?

Schweitzer even found words of sympathy and understanding for the Communist Rosa Luxemburg, usually regarded in Church circles as an offspring of hell. From the prison letters of this woman, who perished in the Communist rebellions in Berlin, he quotes a passage which makes plain her love of animals and adds the following commentary:

The words: "Blessed are the merciful, for they shall obtain mercy" were deeply understood by this woman. But she did not understand that no spiritual renewal of humanity will come about by the methods of violence. "He who takes the sword will perish by the sword" is a text which found fulfilment in her destiny. How much might this noble soul have given to humanity if she had been content to fight ideas with ideas and to employ only spiritual weapons. . . .

As editor of the *Church Messenger*, Schweitzer performed a real act of rescue for Alsatian Protestantism. In many parishes his journal had to take the place of the pastor himself, for since the clergy of numerous parishes had been dismissed by the new French Government as being friendly to Germany, there were many vacant benefices and the unshepherded parishes were threatened with ruin. Schweitzer addressed them thus:

> Since the Thirty Years' War and the Great Revolution we have not known so much misery and the end of it is not in sight yet. Be faithful and endure to the end. Do not let the Word of God fall into neglect and forgetfulness even though there is no regular preacher in your house of God and your young people cannot be instructed in religion as they should.
>
> As Protestants it is our belief that the church is not built on its pastors but that its existence is rooted in true piety. When the church for the time being is largely put out of action then the home must be so much the more the basis of religion. Family devotions and the religious instruction of the children by the parents must keep alive the spirit of true religion.
>
> In the mission field there have been newly formed churches which remained alive and faithful year after year even though no pastor could be sent to them. May God help our orphaned parishes by raising up God-fearing religiously active laymen and may we thus experience the universal priesthood of believers.

In the summer of 1919, Schweitzer, as he had long feared, was obliged to undergo a second operation, but it also gave him great happiness at the same time to hear that his old Barcelona friends of pre-war days intended to invite him to give yet another organ recital. He scraped together his last resources of money for the journey. Triumph awaited him. His musical friends in Barcelona applauded the Strasbourg organist not only out of old affection for him; it seemed to them that his playing had become more spiritual and pure. His patient practising on the tin-cased piano of Lambaréné, on the wooden table in Garaison, and on the harmonium in St. Rémy was now bearing magnificent fruit. Schweitzer the distinguished organist had now become Schweitzer the unique organist, whose style of playing, free from all virtuosity and artifice, exalted and purified every hearer.

His greatest joy came through an invitation from the Swedish Archbishop Nathan Söderblom to give the Olaus Petri foundation lectures in the ancient university of Upsala, at Easter 1920. Only one condition was attached: the lectures must deal with the problem of ethics. It sounded as if the Swedish archbishop had guessed that it was just this theme which had preoccupied Albert Schweitzer since the beginning of the war.

The letter from Sweden arrived just before the Christmas festival of the difficult year 1919 and was the most lovely Christmas gift that he could have wished for. He told the Archbishop that as a convalescent he had to keep to a strict diet. Would it not be too great a burden to give him hospitality in such circumstances? The reply from Sweden was: "That is precisely an additional reason for your coming. You will get better with us. We will look after you and see that you get well."

The ancient city of Upsala, with its red sandstone buildings, its gentle river lined with birch-trees, its libraries and churches, and the crowds of eager-hearted young people streaming in from all parts of Sweden, gave to Schweitzer the feeling that he still had unused energies, and was still young and alive with vital productive powers.

In Nathan Söderblom, militant, cheerful, keen, surrounded at home by a troop of happy children and in his episcopal office by a number of enthusiastic helpers, Schweitzer found a professional theologian after his own heart. And in the students before whom he expounded the problems of world- and life-affirmation he found the ideal audience. When in his last lecture he described the vision vouchsafed to him in the African jungle and put forward his thesis of "Reverence for Life" as a new departure for philosophical thought, he saw how strongly his idea, hitherto cherished only by himself and his wife, impressed and affected others.

Strengthened in body and mind, he now began to think seriously once more of returning to Lambaréné and reconstructing his hospital. He spoke about this to Söderblom, and of the debts he had contracted in order to keep the hospital going in war-time. Söderblom saw at once that it was chiefly this financial difficulty which prevented the resumption of the great work in the African jungle, and started to organize a lecture and recital tour for Schweitzer, who was everywhere gladly received by audiences eager to give money for his distant hospital. The concert halls were always over-flowing.

Baroness Lagerfelt, who later was to work with Schweitzer in Lambaréné, has most impressively described how on his tour through Sweden Schweitzer not only collected money for the rescue of the African brethren but at the same time saved many old Swedish village organs.

At that time the Swedish crown stood high in value as compared with the German mark, and many parishes thought that then was the time to do a good stroke of business by acquiring a German mass-produced organ. But Schweitzer was often able to prevent that.

> Our guest really covered the whole of the country (wrote the baroness), he did not content himself with visiting the big towns only, to which everyone goes, but he managed to get to the most distant spots.
>
> He played in those white churches which stand on the shores of blue lakes in the middle of enormous forests. No foreign artist or traveller had previously even suspected their existence. But now under the arches of these churches the old organs gave forth their sound as never before. Struck with astonishment and

admiration people whispered to each other: "Is that really our old organ? What marvellous tone comes from it all at once."

The Swedish trip was a complete success. Schweitzer now accepted invitations to go to Switzerland and Denmark, to England and Czechoslovakia, in order to give lectures and to play the organ and collect money for Lambaréné. In Germany, France, and Belgium, on the other hand, he refused to "beg", as he termed it, for such countries had suffered too severely from the war and ought rather to employ their resources for reconstruction work in their own land.

On these journeys the wandering lecturer, clad in a rough woollen coat, carried around with him a big bag. It contained many small money bags which betrayed their contents by a label. The doctor had grown accustomed to separate the many various currencies which he had to carry with him by putting them into small white linen purses with labels like "French francs", "English pounds", "Swedish crowns", "Dutch guilders". If people teased him about it, saying it looked far too rustic a procedure, he would answer:

> Once in Paris I was so absorbed in my thoughts that I went further than my ticket allowed. Soon the ticket inspector came along and accused me of attempting to cheat. He declared that I should have to pay a fine. I refused to enter into any explanations but whether I liked it or not took my little purse with its French francs out of my pocket. You should have seen the reaction of the other passengers. They gave it the inspector good and proper. "How can you punish the man?" they shouted. "Don't you see that he comes from the country and doesn't know anything?" I was then allowed to proceed unpunished.

But it was not only as a lecturer and organist that Albert Schweitzer gained an international reputation in post-war Europe. Once again he became increasingly successful as a writer. At the instigation of Archbishop Söderblom, who had been fascinated by the stories of his guest on the subject of his African experiences, a Swedish publisher approached the doctor and requested him to collect and publish in book form the material which hitherto he had scattered in accounts to his friends. The result was the publication of *On the Edge of the Primeval Forest.*

Apart from this book, which was intended for the wider public, Schweitzer was now at last able to finish the first two volumes of his *Philosophy of Civilization*, based on the manuscript despatched from Lambaréné by the American missionary Ford.

His lecture tours and writing had claimed the attention of Schweitzer to such an extent that he had had to give up his posts in the Strasbourg hospital and the St. Nicholas church. He built for himself and his wife a little house at Königsfeld in the Black Forest which it was a delight to them to furnish and arrange as their first real and purely private home. But how dejected they were when they thought about the next stage of their lives. For without much discussion they had reached the decision that Schweitzer should first return alone to Lambaréné. The state of Helene's health and little Rhena's youth made the decision appear the only right one.

CHAPTER 16

The Prose of Africa

SCHWEITZER PAINTED THE letters "A.S.B." on his chests and trunks, signifying "Albert Schweitzer-Bresslau". Although for health reasons his wife could not go with him to Africa this time, her maiden name Bresslau at least accompanied him.

As he prepared to go to Lambaréné he began to be asked if he could not leave his medical work to the official "colonial doctors". His view was that the State alone can never accomplish humanitarian work. All humane endeavours by their very nature are the concern of society and the individual. In any case the State can only send such doctors as it has at its disposal. There must also be doctors who volunteer to serve, and shoulder the burden of the dangerous climate and the alienation from home and civilization in their outposts.

The state of Europe itself was another objection raised to Schweitzer's return to Africa. To this he had a convincing reply:

> Truth has no times and seasons. It is always timely and above all is it so when it seems most untimely. Concern about suffering that is near is very compatible with concern about distant suffering when together these anxieties jolt men out of their thoughtlessness and awaken a new spirit of humanity among men. Also do not say: if the brotherhood of suffering for the time being sends out one doctor here, another there, what is that in comparison with the total mass of suffering in the world?
> From my own experience and also from that of all colonial doctors I would answer that a single doctor out there with the most modest means can be of vast significance to a great many men. The good which he is able to do exceeds a hundredfold the

In his office at Lambaréné; where letters arrive from all parts of the world: and (*below*) with one of the hospital's European nursing sisters

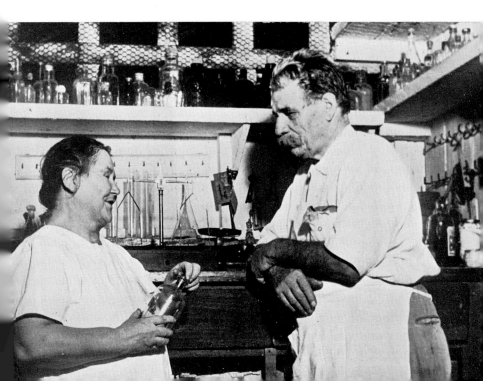

Augustus John makes a sketch of Schweitzer in London, 1955

With Sir Anthony Eden at 10 Downing Street. Earlier in the day
Schweitzer had received the Order of Merit from the Queen

cost in personal self-sacrifice and the financial resources which are made available for his maintenance.

It is just those rapid strides forward which tropical medicine has made in the last fifteen years which puts into our hands an almost miraculous power to heal the great suffering and sorrow of men in distant lands. Is not all this a challenge to us? (From *On the Edge of the Primeval Forest.*)

The fact that this appeal was really listened to, that it was supported by an increasing number of people, and not only by their gifts but also by their personal initiative and energy, gave Schweitzer the strength which he needed in the coming months and years for his struggle against the "prose of Africa", as he liked to describe the very unromantic realities of the jungle.

Pastor Wyatt, Frau Emmy Martin, and Charles Michel in Strasbourg, Pastor Hans Baur, Dr. K. Karcher, J. Fr. Dinner-Obrist, and Frau Emmy Hopf in Switzerland gathered round them an ever-increasing circle of friends. Soon they published a small news-sheet in German, which was sent to Schweitzer's friends with the inscription "Private, please". During the ensuing years it gave information not only about Lambaréné and the struggle against disease under jungle conditions, but also about the gifts of people who had heard of Schweitzer's work. Sometimes it was a young teacher who gave her first month's salary, at other times convalescents or people whose lives had been saved by a successful operation: with a minimum of organization the fellowship of those linked by suffering developed.

On February 21, 1924, Schweitzer again left Europe, by the Dutch cargo vessel *Crestes*. In the last months of 1923, when the inflation was at its height, he had had to correct the proofs of his book *Civilization and Ethics* at night. They arrived late from a north Bavarian printing house which was overworked by the production of millions of currency notes. He also brought out a small subsidiary work which was to go through more editions than any of his other books: the charming and richly significant reminiscences, *Memoirs of Childhood and Youth*. This owed its origin to a suggestion from the Zürich pastor and psycho-analyst Dr. Oskar Pfister, who recognized that Schweitzer's personality was so full and deep that it could not be reduced to any one psychological formula.

Schweitzer hoped that during the voyage he might deal with his heaped-up correspondence, which was contained in four big bags; but the first part of the voyage was excessively cold, because the heating system failed to work, and a loud hammering filled the ship almost incessantly, while old rust was beaten off the plates so that new paint could be put on.

Schweitzer was accompanied by an eighteen-year-old Englishman of Alsatian extraction, Noel Gillespie, who wished to help him during the first difficult months. After a short detour to the former German colony of the Cameroons they lay to at Cape Lopez, the old and now very familiar harbour at the mouth of the Ogowe, now called Port Gentil. The news that "le Docteur" had come back soon spread, and many people ran after him excitedly in the streets to embrace him and kiss his hands.

As he went on up the river, Schweitzer saw that things had not improved since he left the country. Many a village which was still flourishing when he last saw it was a heap of ruins. Spanish influenza, the pressure of hunger, and sleeping sickness had taken a terrible toll here since 1917. The wood-merchants on board the river-steamer confirmed Schweitzer's impression. Certainly wood prices were rising, but the workmen were no longer the same as formerly. Before the war the white man stood high in their esteem, now he had lost his prestige. Colonial soldiers returning to their native villages had told stories to incredulous and astonished audiences about the piles of corpses which were heaped up in the struggle on the Western Front. Africa, too, was in a ferment.

The worst thing of all was the new society of "leopard men". The rise of this mysterious new cult was a constant topic of discussion among the white men. Its members lived under the delusion that they really were leopards, and killed their victims by claw wounds in the arteries of the neck. Members brewed a magic potion from the blood of a murdered man, mixed it in a human skull, and secretly mingled it with the food of an elected person. Only after the event did they tell the victim what they had done. Incapable of resistance, he resigned himself to his fate.

Schweitzer's fellow passengers on the *Alembe* described to him the frightful horrors committed by these animals in human disguise who crept about on all fours. In some places nobody dared to stir abroad after dark. No one felt safe. Such conversations aroused unpleasant surmises in Schweitzer's mind, but the scenery of the primeval forest bathed in moonlight looked as splendid and entrancing as ever.

And then suddenly Lambaréné emerged round a bend in the river. So far as he could see when they entered the tributary of the Ogowe, the doctor's house was uninjured. The three hills with their white buildings were still there. But on landing he saw the tall grass and thick bramble bushes, and the site deep in undergrowth. The main building had all sorts of plants shooting up through its floors, and the entrance to the consulting-room was blocked by a thorn-bush. The former dispensary appeared to serve as a refuge for snakes. But at least the walls were still standing.

Albert Schweitzer arrived for his second period in Africa on Easter Saturday, 1924. On Easter Monday the first sick people came for treatment. Those who came insisted on sleeping at the hospital, as they had been accustomed to do. But their relatives would not lift a finger to help Schweitzer build. Every morning he found patients lying wet through on the damp floor. Sometimes by means of drums he advertised a promise of gifts to people who would help with the most necessary building and repair work, but more often nobody came at all, and then he and Noel Gillespie were left to get on with the job alone.

By dint of pressure Schweitzer tried to coerce the people

into giving promises of helping later with the work, or delivering materials for building—even threatening that only those who brought tiles would get the new remedy for ulcers. When Schweitzer proposed to start making bricks himself for the foundations of the collapsible corrugated-iron hut he had brought with him from Europe, the people ran away from him and went fishing. Schweitzer began to dream about bricks at night. He dreamt of himself as Pharaoh in the Bible, or as an Egyptian taskmaster driving the people of Israel to work, and thus bringing down upon himself the scourge of the ten plagues. Finally he had to admit defeat. He groaned in a family letter:

I have just been called out to a negro village on the other bank of the river, in order to attempt to revive a new born child. I find it naked and ice cold, covered with all sorts of weeds and leaves, lying in the hands of the old women. After an hour and a half, I manage to bring it to the point of breathing correctly. And at once I extort from the father the promise of 500 tiles to be delivered within 14 days as payment.

I find that my moral sense is really beginning to decline. Just as when a child I would ask every aunt who came to visit us whether she had got something for me, so now I snatch the chance of getting from everyone who has any dealings with me, tiles and so forth. It is my dream to have done with building and to be allowed once more to be a doctor, no longer to have to extort tiles from all and sundry, no longer to be a taskmaster driving people from their porridge pots to their work, and having to detect and foil all the little tricks by which they try to escape their "corvée". But it will be a long time before that day arrives.

This *cri du cœur* was dated October 1924. Never before had he expressed himself with such bitterness about Africans or shown himself so dejected. He reached the depths of despair when Noel Gillespie departed, according to plan, at the end of August in order to resume his studies at Oxford. Fortunately in October his place was taken by Dr. Victor Nessmann, the son of an Alsatian pastor, and not long afterwards there arrived at Lambaréné a young woman sent out by friends in Strasbourg to assist him. This was Sister Mathilda Kottmann;

imperturbably calm and always good-humoured, she was for many years one of Schweitzer's most tireless and indispensable helpers.

Another old acquaintance returned to Lambaréné—Joseph, Schweitzer's first medical assistant, the man who had left him during the war because his salary had to be decreased. N'Kendju, the faithful African whom Schweitzer made his second assistant in order to save him from the vengeance of his fellow-tribesmen, was still unfortunately missing in spite of all investigations. The new second assistant was called G'Mba, and Schweitzer was very pleased with him, but he had not the least understanding of order and cleanliness. He could never manage to persuade the women to take their refuse to the rubbish-dump.

It had now become almost impossible to keep any sort of order in the hospital. The reason was that since the doctor's return his patients belonged to quite different tribes from those whom he handled in the years between 1913 and 1917. They were men who had been brought to the Ogowe from the interior in order to work in the lumber camps. The lumber merchants were luring more and more of these Bendjabis to the Ogowe. Most of them could stand neither the unaccustomed food nor the moist heat of the forest. While formerly it was not difficult for the doctor and his assistants to make themselves understood in the three current native dialects, it was now almost impossible for them to communicate with their patients, among whom no fewer than fifteen different dialects were spoken. What a hopeless undertaking it was to impart to these patients the most elementary morality! They stole the doctor's precious building-planks and burned them. They even took food from the sick, and of course every night they tried to break into the hen-house. Schweitzer had the forehead, breast, and back of those thieves he caught painted with the figure of a bird in methylated spirit. At first they took it as a great joke. Later the method seemed to have some effect.

In 1925 something occurred that Schweitzer had foreseen.

A terrible famine spread over the whole Ogowe district. The hospital was to some extent spared, since the doctor had taken care to provide for this lean period by the timely purchase of great stores of rice. Almost at the same time a severe epidemic of dysentery broke out around Lambaréné, which meant constructing some cubicles for dysentery cases by means of temporary wooden partitions within the large main ward. It was almost impossible to induce these contagious patients to observe elementary caution and the rules of cleanliness. Their relatives often brought them river-water infected with dysentery bacilli instead of drawing water from a pure source a little further on, but in spite of such apparently callous negligence it was touching to see how these patients kept together. When a Bendjabi suffering from foot-sores discovered a comrade among the dysentery patients, he gladly entered the isolation quarter in order to cook and sleep with his friend. "I would rather be with my brother and die than not see him," one of them remarked.

While the dysentery epidemic was snatching away so many lives, Schweitzer received an invaluable assistant in the person of the very efficient Swiss surgeon, Dr. Mark Lauterburg. The Africans called him Dr. N'Tschinda, which meant the "courageous carver". His operations made him famous far and wide. Even amputations, which normally Africans were extremely reluctant to submit to, were gladly accepted from Lauterburg, if only he explained to them at sufficient length that he could thereby save their lives. Another nursing sister arrived also: Emma Hausknecht, who contrived to bring a sense of order and peace to Lambaréné.

In the middle of October 1925, a decision which Schweitzer had been long pondering suddenly matured. For some time he had entertained the idea of building a far bigger hospital village about a couple of miles up the river on a site where had stood the village and palace of the sun-king N'Kombe. Once more he went up the river to the site—a broad depression of ground adjoining the river, overlooked by gently rising hills on which the buildings could be erected. The spot was ideal. In all secrecy and without communicating his purpose to anyone he secured leave from the district official to build on an area covering about 172 acres.

When he told the staff there was a burst of applause. Schweitzer then wrote to Europe:

> But I am thinking of the sacrifice which my wife and child must make on account of the removal of the hospital. They are expecting me back home by the close of the winter. And now I shall hardly be able to reach Europe before the beginning of next autumn. Building cannot go on without me. (From *More from the Primeval Forest*.)

CHAPTER 17

The Master Builder in the Wilderness

ON THE WALL of one of the buildings on the new Lambaréné hospital site Albert Schweitzer wrote with a wooden stick on the still soft mass of cement:

> A. Schweitzer, engineer
> A. Schweitzer, mason
> A. Schweitzer, carpenter.

He might well have added that he was also land surveyor, master of land clearing, inspector of works, and architect. In the building of the new hospital village Schweitzer again displayed his drive and energy. With only a handful of chance helpers and weary followers, he built for himself paths through the wilderness with only human muscles, courage, and endurance to carry on the struggle.

Schweitzer now spent his time almost exclusively on the new building site. The doctors and sisters in the old hospital only called him in for specially difficult cases. By means of vouchers, which could be exchanged later for spoons, mugs, plates, knives, cooking-pots, sleeping-mats, rugs, stuffs, mosquito nets, or the much-coveted pocket knives, the doctor provided the necessary inducement for labourers, who in spite of all eloquent arguments refused to understand why they should be expected to build a house which was intended only for future patients, and from which they themselves would hardly be able to profit.

This fifty-year-old man now stood during a ten-hour day in the midst of the wilderness. He often thought of Goethe's *Faust*, for whom the poet assigned as "his last objective that he should win land from the sea, where men could dwell and find sustenance". A few years later, when he was awarded the Goethe prize offered by the city of Frankfurt, Schweitzer confessed: "And thus Goethe stood by me in the gloomy heart of the jungle smiling at me with comfort and understanding."

And Beethoven too, an old friend, is with the doctor when he spurs on the refractory workers, when he hears their voices, their shouts, their spades, and the changing rhythms of their work. For Schweitzer the musician a normal working day runs its course like a symphony, provided that he is in the right mood and does not have to give vent to his anger and bitter words:

Lento : In a surly mood the workmen receive their axes and bush knives which I distribute as they land. At a snail's pace they proceed to the spot where bushes and trees are to be cut down. Finally they have taken up working positions. The first strokes are made cautiously.

Moderato : Axes and bush knives are now working at a quite moderate pace. The symphony conductor tries in vain to accelerate the tempo. The pause for lunch brings the tedious movement to an end.

Adagio : After a painful effort I have succeeded in bringing the workers once more to their positions in the murky forest. Not the slightest breath of air is stirring. From time to time you hear the stroke of an axe.

Scherzo : A few jokes, which I rouse myself from my despair to make are successful. This enlivens the general mood. Merry quips fly to and fro. Some people begin to sing. It is also getting somewhat cooler now. A gentle breeze from the river steals into the thicket.

Finale : All minds are at length attuned to a mood of gaiety. Now it will go badly for the lowering forest, because of which they have to stand here instead of being able to sit peacefully in the hospital. Shrieks of wild curses are heard against it. Howling and screeching, they grapple with its body. Axes and bush knives gash and tear it in rivalry. But now no bird may fly forth, no squirrel may show itself, no question may be asked, no order given. The slightest distraction would break the spell. Axes and bush knives would cease to work and folk would begin to chatter about what had been seen or heard, and the game would be up.

Fortunately there is no distraction. The raging and rending goes on. If this finale can only continue for a good half hour then the day is not lost. And it does keep up until I call out *"Amani, Amani"* (Enough, enough) and the day's work comes to an end. (From *More from the Primeval Forest.*)

Gradually the land for the new hospital village was cleared and made suitable for tilling. Banana shrubs, maize, and bread-fruit slips began to sprout on the soil that had been reclaimed. The construction of the buildings themselves was then planned. On the basis of his experience of tropical Africa, Schweitzer had thought out a special design for a house which represented a curious mixture of the prehistoric and the most modern styles. The roof was to consist of the latest type of corrugated sheet iron, the joists of hardwood, and the whole structure was to rest on piles, as was the case with river and lakeside settlements in the most primitive times.

First came the search for suitable piles, then the digging of holes and the walling them up. The piles had to be hardened by patient charring. The doctor would come home with scorched hands and a coal-black face, until at last he had prepared four hundred of these piles. First, a shed for the builders, then the ramming in of piles for at least five buildings, and after that the real building process could begin. Schweitzer longed for a builder colleague. This time his wish was fulfilled with astonishing speed. Like a godsend, a capable Swiss from St. Gallen, by name Hans Muggensturm, arrived in April 1926, before the dry season which was so important for building work. He set to work in a burst of enthusiasm, and even succeeded in carrying the Africans with him.

In fact the new buildings were almost ready by the approach of autumn for their interior equipment and furnishing. First of all the outside walls were painted by Schweitzer, his medical colleagues, and the sisters. Dr. Trensz, the new doctor from Europe, joined in the work like everybody else.

To be not only an academic specialist, but also to be capable of manual labour, is what the spirit of Lambaréné requires.

There the sisters on one day bandage a fracture with the utmost care, and the next come to the rescue in the work of forest clearing. In the morning they have to feed hens, and in the afternoon they will probably be shooting a boa constrictor. Schweitzer's faithful friends and helpers Mathilda Kottmann, Emmy Hausknecht, and Gertrud Koch could, if they had time, write a fine book packed with reminiscences of Lambaréné—but they have no time.

And so finally at the beginning of 1927 the village of mercy, the small collection of new hospital buildings, has progressed so far that the removal from the old hospital to the new can be begun. January 21 is the great day. The operation cases and the seriously ill are put on stretchers; those with sores and ulcers who are unable to walk are carried on the backs of their wives or husbands; one man blinded by the scourge of sleeping sickness gropes his way forward on the arm of a nurse, while a group of leprosy patients cheerfully join the procession to the landing-place where canoes and motor-boats are waiting, lent by white patients.

With cries of delight the patients beheld the bright and airy new wards, which even had wooden floors in place of the damp trodden earth in the old barrack-like place. The old hospital still had to be pulled down, the beams removed and the nails straightened out. Then the new doctor's residence had to be built on the new site, subsoil water searched for, and another well dug. Paint, paint, paint! The narrow sides of the hospital exposed to the sun had to be coated with oil-colours. The private house for the white patients, who were continually increasing in numbers, was only half built . . . there was never any end to it.

Schweitzer had intended to be back at home for Christmas, 1926, at the latest. But now it was January, then February, then March 1927.

"The painting is taking longer than I thought," he wrote home. "But I am not going to get excited any more. Whether my journey home is a month earlier or later, the main thing is to keep one's blood cool."

In April 1927, he had been living in Equatorial Africa, separated from his wife and child, for a full three years. He complained about the tiredness of his eyes. Tropical anæmia was again making itself felt.

Finally at the end of July 1927 everything was complete. The new hospital village was fully built. It had isolation quarters for cases of sleeping sickness, dysentery, and mental illness. There were sheds for food and stores and medicines. The doctors and nurses were quite wonderfully housed for Equatorial African conditions. Even a boat-house had been built, and the most important building in the village, the main part of the hospital, with its rooms for consultation and treatment, now had two operating theatres, a laboratory, a room for surgical dressings and bandaging material, and a medicine room. In the operating theatre there hung a portrait of Carl Ludwig Schleigh, the discoverer of local anæsthesia.

Now once more the hour of farewell had struck. With how much lighter a heart than in 1917 did the doctor this time take his departure, accompanied by Mathilda Kottmann, the good angel of Lambaréné. He knew that his work now rested on firm foundations and was in good hands. His friends in Europe were providing for regular relays of doctors and nurses. They collected the necessary money and were tireless in giving themselves. He had sufficient supplies of medicine and stores of food, and a splendid new helper, the Canadian Mrs. C. E. B. Russell, organized the division of labour.

When in the late summer of 1927 Schweitzer returned to Europe after his three-and-a-half years' stay in Africa he felt at first strangely homeless. For a new rector now lived in the parsonage at Günsbach, which had been familiar for so many years as his parents' home. Schweitzer's father had died fifteen months earlier, only a few weeks before the jubilee of his ministry there. For Schweitzer it seemed very odd that suddenly he no longer had a home in Günsbach. He felt as though one root of his life had withered. For Königsfeld in the Black Forest he could not form such a deep inward attachment as for the tiny hamlet in the Münster valley.

It was almost a shock to him to find that the personality suggested by his writings, the name printed on his books, had in the meantime not only persisted, but become even more famous. There was admiration for the universal scope of his genius. It was apparent that each of his manifold gifts received support and stimulation from the others, and that in an age of ever-increasing specialization, here was a man capable of sitting upright in many saddles. Schweitzer knew how to surprise the intellectuals by the disclosure of an unsuspected aspect of his rich personality. If, for example, the learned professors sitting round the table at a hotel after a lecture began to bore both him and themselves, he would immediately fish out of his bag an African fetish, and amuse the whole table with gruesomely comic stories to charm away academic tedium.

Another constantly growing group of people venerated Schweitzer—those who were looking for some ground of assurance, faith, and hope. They perceived plainly enough that, in a period of party strife and the clash of egoisms, of covetousness and envy, of careerism, or brutal pushfulness, he had performed an unselfish work of love in Africa, which was a luminous exception to the spirit of the age. They saw in him one of the few righteous men for whose sake Sodom and Gomorrah might have been saved. In the heart of the thick jungle of civilization where opinions and words, ambiguities and contradictions are rampant, he had cleared a piece of ground on which he had built the outlines of his life and thought. Although Albert Schweitzer might be important for Africa it seemed increasingly clear that he was still more important as a warning and a luminary held up to a doubting and decadent Europe. In Lambaréné he healed sick bodies, in Europe he led many sick souls into the way of regeneration.

Dressed in his old clothes, wearing his rough, shabby woollen coat, always with the same crumpled hat on his shaggy hair, he travelled third class through Europe, England, and Scotland, collecting money for his work, receiving honorary doctorates and the freedom of cities. In a town in Switzerland, one of the organizers of the party apologized that he had been unable to secure a room with hot and cold water. Schweitzer replied: "Doesn't matter. I am no trout."

All the money which Schweitzer got from his lecture and recital tours he allocated to Lambaréné, which required ever greater financial support because the number of his patients was constantly increasing. But he used the Goethe prize money, which he was awarded by the city of Frankfurt in 1928, to build himself a home of his own in Günsbach, to house his books and his treasures, and to serve as a centre for his medical colleagues and nurses when they were on European leave. He also rented from the parish of Günsbach a jutting crag of the Kanzelrain which lies on the road between Günsbach and Münster, for the nominal payment of one mark a year. On this peak he loved to sit as a young man, and there he delighted to rest his eyes on the beautiful view of the happy valley which was the scene of his childhood.

CHAPTER 18

An Oasis of Peace

ON HIS THIRD journey to his second home in Africa,
Schweitzer found that under the supervision of his doctor
friends and devoted voluntary nursing staff his hospital village
was not only being maintained but was making further important progress. Lambaréné, his child, his creation, had
learned to make rapid strides forward even when he was not
there. Like a fond father, he noted the fact half with pride and
half with unconfessed regret. Never before had so many
patients been operated on—in one single year the number of
serious surgical interventions had doubled to the number of
nearly five hundred. Never before had the patients travelled
so far from the interior to find release from their suffering in
the hospital by the Ogowe.

There were pumps and wells now, even a bathroom with two
cement baths, a refrigerator, and a wonderful bell sent from
Alsace, which in the evening marked the hour of bedtime and
on Sundays called the patients to prayer. A ward for tubercu-
losis patients, a dining-hall, a wing with visitors' rooms, better
isolation cells for the mentally sick, a special ward for serious
cases, another in which women in labour and babies are looked
after; the village of mercy now had forty buildings.

The establishment of a maternity department was due to the
inspiration of Helene Schweitzer. She wished to see created in
the primeval forest what she had once suggested and carried
through in Strasbourg: a home for orphan children, and also a
place where native women, discarding the taboos and superstitions of their environment, could have their babies. The
abnormally high infant mortality in the area soon receded,

and it was a sign of increasing confidence that more and more mothers went to the hospital as soon as they suspected the beginning of labour. The new-born baby's face was painted white to scare away evil spirits. Schweitzer was shrewd enough not to fight against that tradition, and he usually asked himself about painting the child as soon as a new birth was announced.

Before Schweitzer's time came to return from his third period in Africa his wife was obliged to return to Europe. Schweitzer himself planned to go home more frequently in order to be with his family; between 1932 and 1939 he went to Europe four times, each time with increasing anxiety about the destiny of the world. For since November 1929 his gloomy presentiments became more distinct, and with each passing year received plainer confirmation. When he received the invitation to give the Festival Speech at Frankfurt, March 22, 1932, on the occasion of the hundredth anniversary of Goethe's death, he at first declined, for he felt that other Goethe scholars and research workers were more competent to speak about this prince of poets. But since the authorities of the old Imperial city insisted on hearing the voice of Schweitzer, he decided to make the journey, and on his voyage to Europe wrote perhaps the most profound and beautiful of all his speeches, which sounded like a warning before the temporary submerging of Europe in darkness.

Germany lay under the shadow of an economic crisis. The numbers of unemployed had reached many millions. Fighting in town halls and in the streets made it clear that the country was actually if not officially in a state of civil war. Everybody was short of money, and not least important was the fact that cultural life was beginning to feel the effects of the crisis just in the Goethe festival year. But more than the material distress which everyone was talking about, Schweitzer was moved by the spiritual distress of his fellow creatures. Individuals had to a large extent lost not only their economic but also their intellectual freedom.

Honorary Doctor of Laws, Cambridge, 1955

At the organ of the Royal Festival Hall, London, 1955

Schweitzer grappled vigorously with this tragic situation, which was ignored by most of the other Goethe festival speakers. A year before the inauguration of Hitler's Reich, he said at Frankfurt:

> Our situation which every day is becoming more unnatural is evolving towards the stage when in every respect man will cease more and more to belong to nature and himself, and will be increasingly subjected to the control of society. Hence arises the question which a few decades ago we would have dismissed as absurd: is there any point in still clinging to the ideal of personal humanity when events are moving in such a way as to deny that ideal, or on the contrary are we not bidden to adopt a new ideal of humanity which would suggest a quite different fulfilment of life, through the absolute merging of the individual in the mass of organized society? And what does that mean but that like Faust we go dreadfully astray from the path of nature and surrender ourselves to the dark forces of the unnatural?
>
> After all what is it that we are experiencing in these cruel times but a gigantic repetition of the Faust drama on the stage of the world? The cottage of Philemon and Baucis is going up in a thousand flames! In manifold deeds of violence and in manifold forms of murder dehumanised man is carrying on his wanton sport! Under a thousand grimacing masks Mephistopheles is leering at us! In all sorts of ways humanity has to bring itself to the point of giving up its natural relation to reality and of seeking its salvation in the magic formulas of social-economic blueprints, which only make more remote the possibility of deliverance from economic and social distress!
>
> And the sinister meaning of these magic formulas, to whatever particular social-economic gospel they belong, is always the same, namely that the individual must surrender his material and spiritual independence and can exist only as the member of some multiple entity which claims complete material and spiritual domination over him.
>
> Goethe could not foresee that there would come a time when in this way economic industrial circumstances would work out in the utter elimination of the substantial independence of the individual.

Standing on the stage of the Frankfurt Opera House on March 22, 1932, Schweitzer felt uneasy about the solemn awestruck faces which gleamed up at him like phantoms in the half-light. He spoke without a manuscript. There was not even a desk in front of him, and consequently many felt a personal challenge in his words.

> Never surrender the ideal of personal humanity even when it seems to be negatived by the actual shape of things. . . . Remain men with a living soul. Never sink to the level of human things which allow themselves to be indwelt by a soul focussed on the will and consciousness of the mass and beating in rhythm with it. . . . And may we—for this is the decisive thing—each in so far as in us lies, energize in living deed the sheer noble humanity of "Let man be magnanimous, generous, and good," so that the aspiration does not remain a mere thought but becomes powerfully embodied among us.

Twelve years later, a symbol of the failure of a whole generation, the Opera House was a burnt-out shell, a tangled heap of stone and metal.

After this warning, which at the time was soon drowned in the clamour of Hitler's rallies, for many years Schweitzer did not so much as even indicate his attitude to political developments. He did not append his signature to manifestoes cursing the Third Reich because he did not believe in the effectiveness of such demonstrations. The pessimism of his deep awareness of the total picture presented by man's evolution—a pessimism which he set in conscious opposition to the optimism of his active life—seemed indeed to paralyse him. "My place is not in politics," he said to people who begged him to make his voice heard in protest against what was happening in Germany.

But there can be no doubt about the fact that with all the intensity of his being he repudiated the "new order" in Germany. The fate of his mother-in-law and brother-in-law, who were persecuted as Jews, brought the full horror of the times closer to him than to many others. Friends like the Prague philosopher Oscar Kraus, the tenderly sensitive Stefan Zweig had to suffer and flee. How difficult it was to persuade Stefan Zweig, whom Schweitzer saw in London, that all these terrors would pass away and that one only required the strength to live through these dark years of misery. One rainy day these two men who had known happier days walked together up and down a depressing London street, and already there seemed to gather round them the shadow of grief caused by the later death of Stefan Zweig, and the unimaginable holocaust of millions of other members of his race.

In the years when the swastika waved over Germany, Schweitzer never once wished to visit it or to speak in public there. Official feelers were extended to him from the propaganda ministry. The authorities would have been only too glad to win for Hitlerism the man who had become famous as an exponent of German culture. Once even a letter from Dr. Goebbels came by post to Lambaréné. It contained "with German greetings" a proposal that the forest doctor should once again hold lectures and give organ recitals in Germany. Schweitzer declined with frigid politeness and formally concluded his letter: "With greetings from Equatorial Africa!"

When in January 1939, Schweitzer came again to Europe after a two years' stay in Africa, he persuaded himself, on the basis of the news which he read in the ship's papers and heard on the ship's radio, that war would in all probability break out that year.

And when he landed at Bordeaux he did something unusual: he left his luggage on board the steamer and decided to travel back to Africa by the same boat. Only twelve days remained until the ship's departure, not even a full two weeks, so that he had to make the most of every minute, and to settle his affairs as far as possible before the storm inevitably burst.

By March 3, 1939, Schweitzer was again sailing out of the Bay of Port Gentil into the Ogowe on the river-steamer. This time he left his wife and child behind in Europe with a heavier heart than usual, for he was convinced that war had become inevitable, and that unfortunately the over-clever people who said that at worst only a "lightning war" threatened were just as wrong as they had been in 1914.

During the five months before the outbreak of war
Schweitzer mobilized all his resources. He also felt compelled
to send home a large number of patients who had journeyed a
long way from the interior to get rid of troublesome tumours,
and let them go without operations for the time being; for
surgical supplies had to be kept ready for use in urgent cases.
To the remaining patients the hospital seemed unusually empty
and in fact desolate, for only the seriously ill and the mentally
sick were now treated in it. The Hungarian, Dr. Ladislas Gold-
schmid, who had come to Lambaréné in the thirties as a victim
of racial persecution, and Dr. Anna Wildikann, who managed
to reach Lambaréné from the Baltic provinces after the outbreak of war, were Schweitzer's medical colleagues, and with
the sharp decrease of work in the hospital they had more
leisure than usual.

Yet once again Lambaréné filled up in an almost frighten-
ingly new way. During October and November 1940, a
struggle took place between Vichy French and Free French for
the possession of Gabon. Lambaréné fell within the fighting
zone. Every day aircraft roared low over the forest, artillery
duels were fought out, gunboats were brought into operation,
and regular small battles were waged around various strategic-
ally important points on the river.

The rumour quickly spread among the inhabitants of the
region that Schweitzer had received an assurance from the
leaders of both sides that they would spare his hospital. Hence
whites and blacks with children, and even animals, migrated to
the hospital region, where they found shelter and felt secure in
an oasis of peace. The doctor at once set about strengthening
all the houses which faced the village of Lambaréné, the area of
operations, with corrugated sheet iron. One of the houses was
jocularly called "the panzer cuirass". Lambaréné became like
an ark in the midst of the flood, in which negroes and whites,
Protestants, Catholics, Jews, heathen, cats, dogs, goats, tame
boars, pelicans, anthropoid apes, and antelopes found a resting-
place. Schweitzer, another Noah, was so sure of the meaning

and rationality of his work that he did not seem to be very curious to find out whether the waters had ebbed. The hospital did not possess a radio and the doctor did not even desire to have such an instrument installed. The hospital chiefs learned something of the course of the war only through the type-written bulletin which appeared twice a week. Occasionally a white patient brought a receiving set with him, and expressed astonishment that the doctors and nurses did not seem particularly anxious to be told the latest war news.

But in August 1941 there appeared at Lambaréné an eye-witness of the critical events of the time who reported in dramatic terms the colossal tragedy of the retreat and collapse of France. Rejecting all the advice of her doctors, who counselled her against a further stay in Lambaréné, Helene Schweitzer staked everything on reaching her husband. She left her home in the Black Forest without too much regret. It must now have seemed to her like a presentiment of things to come that she and her husband when they built this home in the year 1923 notched the following proverbs in the beams over the entrance:

> This house is mine and yet not mine
> Nor will he who follows me
> His life therein entwine.

That was one motto. The other ran:

> For we have no abiding city
> But seek one to come.

Helene Schweitzer must often have thought of these wise sayings as with other refugees she fled from Alsace by train, by car, and on foot, in front of the ever-retreating armies and pursued by the screech of low-diving bombers.

After the French armistice of July 1940, Helene Schweitzer went day after day to the temporary government offices in Vichy for a permit to travel to Gabon. Even then a means of travel had to be found. In the spring of 1941 there was no longer any direct communication by sea between Bordeaux and Equatorial Africa, which had surrendered to the Gaullists.

The only European sea passage was that from Portugal. Hence Spanish and Portuguese transit visas had to be first procured, and they were only given when the applicant could show that a passage had been booked. Even this difficulty was eventually overcome. And still there was the dangerous voyage on an overloaded ship and the further slow, tiresome journey by rail and car from the coast to Lambaréné.

During the following years she became in spite of all the difficulties of climate her husband's indefatigable helper. Schweitzer noted:

> My wife takes her turn of duty. Thus it is possible for nurses who have been working without interruption since the outbreak of war to get more rest for the first time. She also takes in hand the preparation and supervision of surgical material, and makes herself useful wherever there is need. Moreover she helps me to deal with my correspondence.

The evil event of war brought into being again the old intimate partnership of Albert and Helene Schweitzer.

Schweitzer wrote about the detached remoteness of Lambaréné:

> Although we are not kept informed about what is going on, we are constantly preoccupied and oppressed by the terrible things that are happening. We are anxious about so many people who are dear to us and who are endangered by these events. We feel ashamed to think that while we here have enough to eat, millions afar off are suffering hunger.
>
> The news of what is happening in prisons and concentration camps, of the persecution of the Jews, and of the sufferings endured by displaced peoples, fill us with horror. The distress of the Dutch, of which we are only bit by bit being informed, moves us deeply.
>
> It is our common experience that every day we must jerk ourselves out of our habitual dejection in order to get on with the tasks that we must perform. All of us feel it as something incomprehensible that while others are condemned to suffer pain or to do things which cause pain and death, we are privileged to have as our vocation compassionate helpfulness. The thought that we are thus favoured gives us daily new strength for our work and makes us feel this work to be something inestimably precious.

On January 14, 1945, Albert Schweitzer was seventy. It is a tradition which Lambaréné had taken over from St. Thomas's seminary that the man whose birthday it is should choose the menu for that day himself. Schweitzer chose roast potatoes, which represent the height of epicureanism at Lambaréné, and are regarded there as a rare dish, somewhat like caviare in Europe.

Tinkling his glass three times with his fork, the big broad-shouldered man with his mane of shaggy grey hair said to his colleagues:

I perceive to my terror that I have been bewitched. The spell arises from the octagonal clock over there which every day is twenty-five minutes late. I too—have been late. And when on November 9 last I was compelled to rest, I understood all at once: you are not sixty-five years old but . . . already seventy. Take your logarithm tables and make a calculation. You will find that it is right.

In these seventy years I have been able to fulfil all my wishes. I am perfectly satisfied with my life. Fate has always favoured me. For example: my work on Kant which was really nothing out of the ordinary my friend Holtzmann recommended to his publisher together with his own works. And instead of having to pay for the printing of this doctorate thesis I have received author's royalties. And thus it has been with me in everything. . . .

And now when I am seventy years old I shall be having my whims and fancies. I shall be wanting to do everything as I think best and people will have to indulge me without requiring long explanations. Then you will be able to say: "It's his age."

My antelope lay waiting for me this morning. I could read in her eyes, "Why must you be always on the go? After all we are two old animals, you and I." I might have explained to her at length the notions of duty and the interdependence of all men. She only looked at me with eyes which seemed to pity my ignorance and to say: "Just look at me and do as I do. I don't even get up when you bring me my food."

I had dreamed of retiring when I reached the age of sixty-five in order to spend at least ten years of my life pleasantly and com-fortably. I had intended to come out here one year as an amateur, so to speak, and then to go for a year to France so as to be able to work quietly at my books between two journeys of pleasure, and look after my wife, child, and grandchild for a bit.

Well, all these schemes were very fine but most unfortunately I now realise that I must not give up and I also foresee that my final years will be much harder and more burdened with duties then my earlier years. All that makes me very sad.

If you were to make a chemical analysis of my soul you would find in it three equal parts: first, one third professor, second, one third doctor, and lastly one third countryman. In addition a few drops of the "primitive man".

And of course from now on the few drops of the "primitive man" will increase. And if you find that it won't do, then do not make a fuss about it. Simply say to yourselves: "The primitive man is getting the upper hand with him."

On the evening of this seventieth birthday they listened to the radio in Lambaréné. The British Broadcasting Corporation transmitted a birthday programme for Albert Schweitzer. With tears of emotion he and his friends were able to listen to the recording of a Bach recital which he had given before the war on an organ in a Strasbourg church. It was a festive conclusion to the great day.

When finally on Monday May 7, 1945, news was received about noon that hostilities in Europe had ceased, Schweitzer hardly had time to rejoice in the fact. For he was just finishing off letters which were to be sent by the river-steamer already waiting for the mail. Not until the afternoon did the great bell ring out, and only then did the inmates of the hospital learn of the great event.

That night he got down a little book containing the maxims of Lao-Tze and read the following words:

Weapons are injurious instruments, not meant for the noble-minded. The noble soul only uses them when he cannot do otherwise. . . . He values tranquillity and peace above all things.

He conquers but he does not rejoice in his conquest. He who would find pleasure in conquering would find pleasure in the murder of men. . . .

In the celebration of victory the leader should adopt an attitude dictated by the customs of mourning. The killing of men in great numbers should be lamented with tears of grief and compassion. Hence the party which has been victorious in the struggle should tarry as over the graves of the beloved.

CHAPTER 19

Halo of Glory

SHORTLY BEFORE HIS seventy-third birthday Schweitzer received a letter from the Basel studio of the Swiss Broadcasting Society telling him that on January 14 a programme would be arranged on the short wave transmitter specially for him. So on January 13, 1948, the doctor heard in the Lambaréné dining-room the bells of the little church in Günsbach, after which five men, five old friends, came to the microphone one after the other in order to address him in his native dialect.

First of all the mayor of Günsbach introduced himself:

> Good day, my dear Albert. I am the mayor of Günsbach. I would never have dreamt that one day I should be sending you birthday greetings and good wishes over the radio thousands of miles across the ocean. But so it is. In such matters the world is making rapid progress indeed.
> You are now seventy-three years old, which means that you are getting on. And the trouble is that you cannot even live in a way suitable to such an age, but must wear out your life in toil, and in a climate of such torrid heat on top of everything else. The men of Günsbach and Grischbach are thinking about you today and wish you all the best, especially good health.
> But I really must tell you one thing. They are all a little cross with you because you are such a long time coming home. That is not right. Do we count for nothing any more? After all you do belong to us, not only to the blacks, though we wouldn't for the world say a word against them. Your seventy-fourth, or at least your seventy-fifth birthday must certainly bring you back home to us. We absolutely insist on that. I must now bring this message to an end. The gentleman in charge has warned me that speaking over the radio is not like speaking on the telephone or at a meeting of the town council. Here one must be brief which I hope I have been. Well, dear Albert, may God have you in His

keeping, don't work too hard and don't forget that you've got to come home on your seventy-fourth birthday. You have heard me, haven't you?

All the speakers struck at Schweitzer's homesickness:

"I, Fritz Koch, wish to tell you that the whole village is very proud of you. I am already much looking forward to the time when I shall be able to go for a walk with you through our vineyards and on the Kanzerain. I do so hope that this will soon be the case. Nor have I forgotten the concert you promised us, I hope we shall soon have the pleasure of hearing it."

"I, Neef, your neighbour and the captain of the fire brigade, tell you quite frankly that there is no child running around in the village under the age of about ten who has ever seen you although they all know you well enough by name."

"I, Arnold, your neighbour, would like you to know that I have looked after your house in difficult days exactly as if it had been my own. For your sake nothing has been too much trouble to me.

"And I, dear Dr. Schweitzer, Ortlieb, the schoolteacher, the last one to speak, would ask you to bear in mind that not only we but also the church and organ are waiting for you. The bells of Günsbach which you have heard under the palm trees were meant to arouse in your heart the nostalgia which you ought to feel."

Whether it was the influence of these nostalgic messages or the fact that in the autumn of 1948 the work at the hospital had once more shrunk to moderate proportions, in any event Schweitzer set sail for Europe on the river-steamer on October 1, 1948. On October 29 he shook hands with the five men who had called him back to Günsbach, and then went on to Mannedorf on the lake of Zürich, where his daughter Rhena was living as the happy mother of four children. Following the family tradition, she had married an organ-builder.

Schweitzer once again had more than enough work in Europe. He worked at the third part of his philosophy of culture, and also kept his eye on Lambaréné affairs. In the middle of one theological discussion with a Basel friend the representative of a well-known Basel chemical firm called to offer the doctor a contribution from his factory. Schweitzer tore himself away from the discussion on genuine or false eschatology to discuss the merits of the new preparation, promin. While that was going on, his friend looked at Schweitzer's manuscript lying on the table. It was written on the backs of old hospital bills, for as Schweitzer explained, "I still consider economy to be a virtue."

The running of Lambaréné had become an expensive responsibility. There were four hundred human beings to feed as well as buildings to maintain. Schweitzer himself insisted, however, that he should have no contribution from countries which had to cope with a difficult refugee problem. To a German friend who wished to organize a collection on behalf of Lambaréné he wrote:

> It is my principle that so long as refugee distress exists in Germany I should do nothing publicly nor allow anything to be done for me in order to receive gifts for my hospital. I must not take away gifts which might alleviate the distress of refugees. I beg you to understand my point of view. I can do no other. I thank you for your willingness to help me.

But there suddenly came to Schweitzer an offer which had to be considered. It was an invitation to make the festival speech on the occasion of the two hundredth anniversary of Goethe's birth at the American resort of Aspen, Colorado; the payment would be 6,100 dollars, with travelling expenses in addition.

With that amount of money Schweitzer knew he could begin to build a new leprosy hospital at Lambaréné. Once more, he thought, Goethe was building him a house, a whole lot of houses.

In the middle of June 1949, the Schweitzers sailed in the *Nieuwe Amsterdam*, and on June 29 Schweitzer saw the statue of Liberty in New York Harbour, sculptured by Bartholdi, whose sad negro on the Colmar monument had once so decisively inspired him. In a very few days the whole of America knew him as "Mr. Corrugated Iron", or as "the thirteenth disciple of Jesus", or simply as "the greatest man in the world".

Aspen, where the two hundredth anniversary of Goethe was to be celebrated, lies high on the Colorado plateau a few hours westwards from Denver. As a silver-mining town its days of prosperity are behind it. It owes its restoration to a millionaire of German origin, Walter Paepcke, a ski enthusiast who was keen on excursions to this lovely spot. He and his wife had taken with them ski teachers who had emigrated from Austria and Germany, built a ski lift, laid down tracks, and set about making Aspen a popular winter-sports centre. They had already instituted a world ski championship at Aspen, and now they wanted to have a summer attraction as well, and so they hit upon the idea of—Goethe.

In the summer of 1949 they collected in this remote mountain spot the great Spanish philosopher Ortega y Gasset, the Italian thinker Borghese, the American poet Thornton Wilder, the German Goethe scholar Professor Bergstrasser, and the chief star in this galaxy of distinguished men, Albert Schweitzer. In addition, there was a whole symphony orchestra under the conductorship of Mitropopulos, and the virtuoso pianist Arthur Rubinstein.

Unfortunately the crisp mountain air did not at all agree with Schweitzer after his many years in the jungle. He suffered from breathing trouble, and only stayed two days. However, the speech which he delivered in French and German in the big circus marquee, his piano-playing in the comfortable little guest house, and especially his tremendous gift of humour and his humanity left behind a deep impression.

People admired above all the cordiality and openness with which this grey-haired man devoted himself to anyone who sought his help, whether it was a famous professor or a simple student. He refused to listen to the pleas of those around him to spare his strength. Schweitzer's comment was, "I must not say no to any human being who thinks that I can help him— even if it were merely by an autograph. It may be that in an hour of distress he will be encouraged by it."

In the following years Albert Schweitzer did not always express himself so charmingly about the inquisitive sensation-hunters who now began to waylay him. For since his American journey he had become world-famous and had to pay the heavy cost of all those who stand in the full glare of public attention.

"I seem to have become a new kind of African elephant. They pursue me with their photo and film cameras as though I were a sort of fantastic wild beast," he once complained to a friend from South Africa, Clara Urquhart. "Not so long ago I literally had to bandy words with some American television men. They just dumped themselves in my hospital and absolutely refused to accept the fact that I categorically declined to appear on a television programme. They treated me as though by my attitude I was repudiating wantonly a sacred duty towards them."

In a letter he wrote from Lambaréné in January 1953 to his friend Richard Kik he said: "I have attained success in life but no one knows how hard my life is and how dearly I pay for this success. In Europe I am a leaf carried away in the eddies of a stream."

Each visit to Europe was now looked forward to with mixed feelings by Schweitzer and his nurses, for it inevitably brought a round of Press conferences, ceremonies, banquets, visits of thanks, hundreds of letters, and autographs. "I wish the doctor were still as obscure as formerly!" one of his loyal women helpers wrote to a Swiss friend.

And yet Schweitzer often feels deeply moved by the genuine love and affection which he is able to evoke in many people.

A refugee wrote him a very beautiful letter: "It is so very good to know that in the middle of a century in which the heart has withered, a Lambaréné is possible and has been embodied in fact."

There are classes in schools dealing with the course of his career; young people's clubs for the protection of animals are founded under his patronage; schools, private boarding-schools, and students' homes wish to be called after him and to work in the spirit of love.

He refuses to hide himself in his house at Günsbach or put notices outside forbidding interruptions. As more and more people travel to Günsbach as to a place of pilgrimage, even rolling up in bus-loads, he gladly shakes their hands, and even plays to them on the organ of the little church. Anyone who calls out a greeting to him as he sits in his room looking out on to the main street can be sure of getting a greeting in return.

In the autumn of 1949 Schweitzer returned to Lambaréné after a short interval in Europe to begin at once on the building of the new leprosy hospital. This time he remained until the spring of 1951. On September 16, in the church of St. Paul at Frankfurt, he received the peace prize offered by the German bookselling trade from the hands of his old friend Theodor Heuss, now President of the German Federal Republic. By December 12 he was back in Lambaréné, where he stayed for the next eight months. At the end of September 1952, Schweitzer, who described himself on that occasion as the lowest type of country doctor, was given the Paracelsus medal of the German Medical Association. In October he was chosen to succeed to Marshal Pétain's seat in the Paris *Academie des Sciences Morales et Politiques*, although he had no time to propose himself or pay the usual candidate's visits. On the occasion of this visit to Paris the reporters discovered that Albert Schweitzer, philosophically the polar opposite of the existentialist Jean-Paul Sartre, was the latter's great-uncle. Schweitzer had at one time pushed little Paul round the Luxembourg Gardens in a pram.

In November 1952, he was presented with the Prince Charles Medal in Stockholm by the Queen of Sweden, and was given the freedom of the cities of Colmar, Kaysersberg, and

Münster, and became Doctor of Laws *honoris cause* of the University of Cape Town and the University of Chicago.

Schweitzer had again and again been proposed as candidate for the Nobel Peace Prize, and in the year 1952 it was confidently expected that he would get it. But it was not until 1953 that the award was made. The doctor was loaded with telegrams, requests for interviews, articles, and radio talks. His reply was:

"Please allow me to get on with my work. I must build my new leprosy village. The 147,000 crowns of the prize are the more welcome to me because I can buy a great deal of corrugated iron with them . . ."

Reporters who came to see him were barked at by his dog Tschutschu.

"Behave yourself, Tschutschu," said Schweitzer. "You are a Nobel dog now!"

A year later Albert Schweitzer went to Oslo for the prize, and had a reception such as had never before been given to a Nobel prize winner. Crowds stood in front of the university for hours in foggy weather in order to get a glimpse of this good man whose life's work was now receiving its outward crown.

In October 1955, in London, Schweitzer was received by Queen Elizabeth and decorated with the Order of Merit. At Cambridge the University awarded him an honorary degree. On two days Schweitzer sat for hours in a small back room in a restaurant in Westminster to meet his British friends. He sat at a table with a shaded light throwing a soft glow over his head and face. The famous people who came included Bertrand Russell the philosopher, Vaughan Williams the musician, and Augustus John the painter. For two days his friends passed by the table to greet him, and the doorway was always thronged by those who had just come "to look at Schweitzer". He wore an old black Alsace clerical jacket, a flowing black tie, and a wide-awake collar. His tumbling grey hair and moustache seemed to be all about his face, curtaining the steady gaze of his eyes. Each visitor who sat by his side had his undivided attention, complete with gesticulations and ready grin. One friend who tried to draw him on Europe's politics was parried with the remark, "I am concerned with ethics."

To-day Lambaréné is no longer the remote village to which Schweitzer went in 1913. It has a small airport, it is the meeting-place of big new roads leading into the interior, and has also become the centre of a new petroleum region. The towers of boring machines can be seen not far from the hospital, and the pumps are working day and night. The primitive oasis which Schweitzer gradually created will no doubt have to yield, within measurable time, to the inevitable progress of technology.

"If you wish to come to my funeral you will have to take the trouble to make the journey to Lambaréné," said Schweitzer to the journalists in Oslo.

He has even thought out an inscription for his tomb. In his merry waggish manner he imagines that his cannibal friends in the heart of Africa might perhaps one day do him the ultimate honour of eating him up. In that event he supposes they would inscribe on his gravestone the epigram:

> *Nous avons mangé*
> *le Docteur Albert Schweitzer*
> *Il a été bon jusqu'à sa fin!*